Reworking Authority

D0819434

- Needs -

Feelings & change
└ the psychological "feel"

- broader & more
strategic understanding
of enterprises & its
purposes p. 4
- a convincing 'theory of
the future' p. 5
- climate that encourages
expenditure of stress,
collaboration, willingness
to share info — vs. fear p. 6
- reliance on "internal
images of themselves —
their own personal authority
p. 9

Organization Studies
John Van Maanen, general editor

Reworking Authority

Leading and Following in the Post-Modern Organization

Larry Hirschhorn

The MIT Press
Cambridge, Massachusetts
London, England

© 1997 Massachusetts Institute of Technology

All rights reserved. No part of this book may be reproduced in any form by any electronic or mechanical means (including photocopying, recording, or information storage and retrieval) without permission in writing from the publisher.

Set in Melior by The MIT Press.
Printed and bound in the United States of America.

Library of Congress Cataloging-in-Publication Data

Hirschhorn, Larry.
  Reworking authority : leading and following in the post-modern organization / Larry Hirschhorn.
    p.   cm. — (Organization studies)
  Includes bibliographical references and index.
  ISBN-13 978-0-262-08258-7 (hc. : alk. paper) – 978-0-262-58173-8 (pbk. : alk. paper)
  1. Leadership.   2. Organizational change.   I. Title.   II. Series : Organizational studies (Cambridge, Mass.)
HD57.7.H56   1997   96-48420
658.4′06—dc21   CIP

10 9 8 7

Contents

Acknowledgments

Many people contributed to the development of this book. Barbara Feinberg, the editor every author hopes for, read each page of the manuscript with her laser-like mind, pointing out, sometimes with no mercy, when my thinking was slipshod. Madeleine Page has been a critical reader of all my works and a challenging co-consultant on many assignments. Howard Schwartz and Ken Eisold gave the original manuscipt a thorough going over, protecting me from my own oversights. Wally Katz helped think of the terms of art that would make my manuscript accessible to a wide range of readers. Fred Block was, as he has been for decades now, a faithful critic and friend. My colleagues at the Center for Applied Research generously supported this work. My wife and companion, Marla Isaacs, contributed to this book and everything else I do. My older son Aaron, in his purposefulness, and my younger son Daniel, in his vitality, remain my inspirations. Finally, I would like to thank all my clients for sharing with me their hopes and their difficulties, and for allowing me to help them.

Introduction: Beyond the Modern Organization

As is evident from the popular and the academic press, and in our own lives, the enterprises we work in—organizations formed and managed to accomplish particular economic and/or social purposes—are under great stress. For some time we have plumbed the roots of this stress, yet we have not understood how our enterprises should respond to it with new and fruitful forms of leadership, supervision, and organizational design.

This challenge stems from what scholars and journalists call "the post-industrial revolution." Propelled by new information and communication technologies, this revolution transforms the conditions by which enterprises create value for their customers, compete with one another, and build and manage their own internal procedures and processes. These new technologies likewise transform how people work, the skills they need, the knowledge they can and should contribute to the organization, and the kinds of careers they can expect. In sum, enterprises now face a less stable and more uncertain market than in the past.

What Business Are You In?

Until about 1950, an enterprise could define its main business with reasonable certainty. Automobile companies were in the business of making and selling cars; electrical utility companies made and distributed electricity; hospitals "produced" health care and "sold" treatment. Today, however, a growing number of enterprises must address a persistent and fundamental question: What business *are* we in? Telephone companies sell basic telephone services, but they also are in the data transfer business and the teleconferencing business—

and they frantically make alliances with other businesses: cable television systems, entertainment conglomerates, and so on. Thus, they are no longer strictly in the telephone business; they are in something more nebulous: the interaction business. Similarly, copier companies may sell copiers, but they also sell information management services, document storage and retrieval services, graphic design services, and publishing services; we can say that they are in the business of organizational memory. And, although a hospital still sells treatment, it also sells preventive medicine, home care, aftercare, and data services for tracking health outcomes. We can say that it is now in the business of patient care management. More significant, for many companies this diffusion of "what business we are in" is widening; indeed, it is not clear where "the business" will take many a firm.

The leaders and the members of an enterprise can no longer depend on an enduring definition of their business, based on a specific product or encounter. As an enterprise takes on broader business objectives, it increasingly *negotiates* the meaning of its business with its customers, competitors, and partners.[1]

Technological Changes

New information technologies integrate disparate activities, enterprises, and individuals—and they do this more closely and more rapidly than before. The hospital that develops a personal-computer-based "health outcome information system" can assess how decisions about primary-care referral affect the course of a patient's stay in the hospital, or how inpatient procedures shape a patient's experience of recuperation. With such information constantly at hand, the hospital can build new ties to the primary-care physicians who refer patients. The hospital pulls these physicians into its orbit of work and planning, so that over time doctors are not only treating patients but also managing their care both before and after they enter the hospital. This new task, in turn, raises new opportunities and threats as the hospital faces its future: Is the hospital now competing

1. Ulrich Beck has argued that new levels of risk and uncertainty define the character of "reflexive modernization," which I am calling "post-modernism." See Ulrich Beck et al., *Reflexive Modernization* (Stanford University Press, 1994).

with primary-care physicians? Are these physicians the hospital's strategic partners in the management of patient care? Will the hospital's incursion into the realm of primary care evoke a competitive response from insurance companies? Will primary-care physicians respond by willingly coming into the hospital's orbit; or will they fund and develop cooperatively owned health outcome information systems; or will they develop new health-related services in social, preventive, or occupation medicine through which they can carve out a new niche for themselves? What business is the hospital in? What do doctors *do* these days?

The new technologies bring in their wake not only new services but also a more complicated set of marketplace relationships in which the traditional lines between the organization and its competitors, suppliers, and customers are less revealing. No wonder many writers describe the new marketplace as a turbulent setting in which the rules of the game change as quickly as the players.

The above changes generate three important and interrelated impacts on employees. First, the enterprise now needs more information, insight, and intelligence to make good decisions—both daily and over the longer run. Second, whereas an employee was once considered a pair of hands, the focus has shifted to the employee's mind. Third, individuals perform fewer rote tasks and instead must make more decisions.

Impact on Employees

Most "platform workers" in banks, for example, traditionally performed simple tasks such as opening new accounts and initiating home loans. Now, operating desktop computers, they introduce customers to new bank products, complete loan applications, and facilitate the electronic transfer of money. These workers do not require more education, although they certainly need adequate technical training and skills in reading and calculating. Rather, they must be prepared to make more choices in the process of helping customers. The worker does not simply follow prescribed protocols; instead, with tools and training, he or she makes more decisions. Daily work becomes more decision-intensive. In this sense, the new enterprise does not push decision making down so much as it *creates new loci* for decision making. These new loci, in turn, help the bank create new value for its customers by adding new services (e.g., mutual funds), thereby further blurring the institution's business. By tracking customers' requests, the workers' responses, and the customers' responses, the bank learns not only about the workers' skills but also about the changing marketplace.

The growth of such "mind work" has flourished in the manufacturing sector. Manufacturers with automated facilities increasingly discovered that their operators had to make more decisions about scheduling work, calibrating instruments, stopping production, monitoring mistakes, and assessing any systematic deviations from the expected quality and quantity of output. Interestingly, in contrast to the earlier anticipation that automation would "dumb down" factory work, just the opposite appears to have happened.

The third impact of information technology is the employees' need for a broader and more strategic understanding of the enterprise and its purposes. In the post-industrial economy, the customers—other companies or consumers—are both scarce and choosy. Each service encounter is thus more valuable; it is both a moment of exchange and a moment for learning about the customer's needs and interests while building the customer's loyalty. Employees at all levels of the organization must learn to look at these encounters as strategic events: What are customers asking for? When and why do they resist our prices? What do they think of our nearest competitors? How can we tell if they are satisfied and if they are not? What do we need to change? In the past, it was heuristically convenient to separate operating the firm from shaping and implementing its strategy. This is no longer possible.

New Relationships between Leaders and Followers

As an enterprise links strategy and operations while the definition of its business becomes fuzzier, its leaders develop a new relationships with their employees. For example, the executives of a large and successful regional hospital spoke of wanting to reduce costs but worried that nurses and physicians would try to block such an effort. As my team of consultants worked with them, we discovered that these executives did not simply disagree with one another about why costs should be reduced; most of them had not articulated any reasons at all. As a result, they had no narrative—no convincing theory of the future—that could persuade their employees to cooperate in a cost-reduction effort. Furthermore, these executives had planned to conduct several conferences for employees on "the future of the tertiary care hospital," but they came to realize that such sessions would be irrelevant unless they addressed the unarticulated narratives of the hospital's future. Why invent imaginary futures for the hospital if the key strategic questions are not first articulated? Moreover, organizing such conferences poses risks to the executive team. What if employees have their own ideas? What if the executives look foolish or do not appear to be in control? Yet if the team did not sponsor such discussions, it faced significant barriers to *acting* strategically.

Coercion and Fear

Why would the executive team of the above-mentioned hospital have to persuade the employees? Why not simply tell them— indeed, order them? In the industrial past, and where unions were absent, employers (particularly those who dominated a local economy) could force workers to work hard physically and at specific tasks. But in today's hospital, for example, senior executives can succeed in guiding the enterprise only if they depend deeply on their employees' skills, their willingness to collaborate with one another, and their ability to recognize the impact of their work on the performance of the enterprise. What would coercion and threats look like in this context? How do you force someone to work hard at making decisions? Since decisions often depend on the ways in which people collaborate, who is accountable for a poor decision? The control systems built up over a century of industrial development are no longer useful in these settings.

To be sure, many executives successfully govern by fear. Employees threatened by job loss will submit to demands to take on more work while accepting less discretion in their activities. But terror has its costs for an organization qua organization. Although cutback strategies help executives reduce costs in the short term, they provide neither vehicle nor framework for developing new sources of revenue. Indeed, much statistical evidence demonstrates that companies that fire employees to cut costs do not boost their profits in the long run. Coming up with organizational redesigns and new customer-employee relationships involves creative thinking; long-term cutback efforts and the climate of fear that cost cutting engenders inhibit such activities and jeopardize long-term profitability.

It is clear in this context that the transition to a post-industrial economy creates its own contradictions. The loss of jobs, the destruction of career ladders, and the obsolescence of skills undermine the ability and the willingness of individuals to collaborate with one another and with the executives who employ them. Anxious about their security, employees are reluctant to share know-how and information with co-workers. Making others look more competent may undermine one's own career chances. And, whereas in the past employees would help one another under the assumption that such favors would be returned, as turnover increases employees are unlikely to be repaid the moral debts owed them. But such a climate of fear does not quash new working relationships completely. Instead, it creates a "force field" in which the constraining forces of fear and dislocation are intertwined dynamically with the enabling forces of shared decision making and the authorization of people at all levels of the hierarchy. This is the new dialectic of the transition to post-industrialism.

Why Post-Modern?

What does the term "post-modern" signify? I used "post-industrial" and "post-industrialism" in describing certain economic and technological changes. Those shifts are well understood by now. Less well understood, however, are their implications for the psychological "feel" and climate of the workplace. If we build new systems of collaboration, decision making, and control, how do these changes shape individuals' experiences of their work and their attempts to make meaning of it? How, if at all, do they revise their intuitive understanding of their relationship to authority, their freedom to act, the nature and extent of their obligations, their relationships with co-workers, and the basis of their competence? In this book I will focus on such questions. I use the term "post-modern" to signify the wish to explore these questions of feel, climate, psychology, and sensibility. Positing that organizations face new kinds of business challenges, I then ask "How does this feel?" and "Do these new feelings, in turn affect the development and effectiveness of the enterprise?"

The Modern Sensibility

In the twentieth century, social scientists, journalists, and cultural critics of art and literature grew accustomed to using the term "modern" to telegraph a conception of a certain psychological and cultural sensibility. In contrast to pre-modern or medieval man, the social scientists and others emphasized, "modern man" had gained the freedom to choose who he married, where he lived, and what occupation he pursued. Faced with such choices, they suggested, people developed a richer inner life. They elevated the role of love in marriage and prized themselves as unique individuals.

In this description, however, we sometimes miss a parallel development. As people became free to choose, they did not just dispose of all authority; instead, they *internalized* authority. No longer responsive to external commands (hence the increasing political attacks on monarchies), they erected internal authority figures— most important, their parents and teachers—who, "in absentia," shaped their choices from within. They developed what David Riesman called an "inner gyroscope" to help guide their decisions in settings that offered many more choices.[2] Just as the early Protestants responded to the voice of God unmediated by the external authority of the priest, modern man constructed a "monarchy" within his psyche. Sigmund Freud referred to this monarchical voice as the person's "superego" (literally "over-I"). One created one's own superego (hence the individual's greater freedom), but one built it out of psychological and cultural materials gathered from one's past and current environments. Thus, freedom was double-edged: a person had greater freedom of choice but also felt greater internal pressure to make particular choices. This ambiguous grant of freedom set the stage for the meanings individuals ascribed to their choices and for the feelings they experienced in making them. It played a special role in shaping the psychological climate of what historians have called the bourgeois or modern family.

Max Weber argued that this new concept of the individual set the stage for the modern capitalistic enterprise. He focused in particular on how the Reformation reshaped individuals' experiences of their

2. David Riesman, in collaboration with Reuel Denney and Nathan Glazer, *The Lonely Crowd: A Study of the Changing American Character* (Yale University Press, 1950).

personhood, their individuality. The sense of the religious calling, the belief that one could have a private relationship with God, and the conviction that one's success in good works (rather than faith or introspection) indicated whether one would be saved all shaped the "character type" that propelled the development of a market society. The ideal-typical Protestant became the capitalist who valued successful work over consumption, focused on the future rather than the present, valued privacy and private property, and committed his efforts to a specialized economic role. New concepts of the self converged with new concepts of production and exchange.

The process of internalizing authority deepened and sustained the impact of the Reformation on character. Freud argued that an individual responds to the actual authority figures in his present life by "transferring" or "projecting" onto them the images of authority figures from his past, which he still carries in his mind. Bosses appear important not simply because they exercise real power, but also because we invest them with the moral authority we once accorded our parents and teachers. This sets the stage for our strivings. The boss's presence stimulates the employee's wish to be like the boss (much as a boy wishes to be like his father), to surpass the boss, to defeat the boss, or to resist the boss. It is this striving that undergirds an employee's ambitions. (I do not discount other sources for these ambitions, but I want to focus on their psychological roots here.)

Many individuals, it was said, expressed these strivings as a desire for upward mobility, as a way of acquiring the resources to be like or to surpass the authority figures in their lives. One's boss and the organization one worked in became, in Howard Schwartz's terms, one's "organizational ideal."[3] Hoping that they would be upwardly mobile, employees internalized the authority of the enterprises in which they worked, as represented by the boss; they identified with the boss in the hope of becoming or surpassing him. The boss, in turn, was well served, since he no longer had to coerce the employees to work hard. Instead, they chose to submit. To be sure, people still worked for "slave wages" in brutalizing settings; however, as union organizers discovered, workers' hopes for upward mobility limited their tendency to identify with their class

3. Howard Schwartz, *Narcissistic Process and Organizational Decay: The Theory of the Organizational Ideal* (NYU Press, 1990).

rather than with the boss. The modern sensibility thus made authority portable. Individuals did not have to be in the presence of actual authority figures in order to feel deeply obligated to do the work required of them.

The New Authority Relationships

If individuals are now working in post-industrial organizations, or if the trend is in that direction, how are their relationships to organizational authority different, and how do these new relationships shape a post-modern concept of personhood? A central hypothesis of this book is that upward identification is no longer sufficient. Because of the wider technological and economic changes enterprise leaders now face and must manage, bosses can no longer project the certainty, confidence, and power that once facilitated employees' identification with them. Employees cannot simply and readily transfer onto bosses the images of authority they internalized when they were young and dependent. This is why people are so disappointed in leaders today but also so unforgiving of them: we resent their failure to live up to our internal images of how powerful they should be.

This dilemma points the way to a possible solution. If individuals are to bring their strivings and passions to their work (as their bosses desperately want), they must now rely more on internalized images of themselves—on an emotional appreciation of who they are, who they wish to become and what they can contribute specifically to an enterprise. *They have to rely in greater measure on their own personal authority.*

Personal Authority

When individuals rely on their personal authority, they bring more of themselves—their skills, ideas, feelings, and values—to their work. They are more psychologically present. It is not uncommon today to find a subordinate heading a task force of which his or her boss is a member. The subordinate must bring greater courage to such a role. Similarly, middle managers responding to requests for "creative undertakings" and "entrepreneurial efforts" find that they must deepen their ability to influence the thinking of others. While they can't just "do their own thing," neither can they simply go along and "not make waves." They have to learn to lead from the middle. An operator in a nuclear power station must follow procedures to the letter while also being prepared for unexpected emergencies, relying on his own judgment and skill and on those of his peers. To take up their roles, individuals must become more resourceful psychologically. This means that a person has to work harder psychologically, learn to take the viewpoints of others, and risk greater shame as more errors inevitably follow in the wake of creative decision making. Yet many individuals feel ambivalent about taking up their personal authority. We now face an extended transition period in which individuals will wrestle with the new challenges imposed by the exercise of personal authority.

The Stresses of the Transition Period

The story of General Motors is revealing in this context. Under the direction of its early leader, Alfred P. Sloan, GM became the paradigmatic modern enterprise, with separate car divisions linked tightly to a headquarters where executives exercised strict financial control over each division. GM also created the paradigmatic culture of the modern enterprise: a culture in which all executives identified deeply with senior management and shaped their career decisions to maximize the chance that they could some day reach the hallowed fourteenth floor (the executive suite) of the headquarters in Detroit.

As many analysts have emphasized, this culture and structure ultimately undermined GM's ability to compete. Intense loyalty to the company once ensured that GM executives would continue to use Sloan's formula for success: exploit the company's sheer size, achieve tremendous economies of scale, and be able thereby to offer a distinct car for each of the income classes. But when this formula failed (in part because of the ability of the Japanese to keep costs low not by building cars in great numbers but by building them more efficiently and with less re-work), this same executive loyalty created an enormous roadblock to developing a new strategy.

As the leaders of General Motors struggled with the limits of their cultural heritage, they abandoned some of the rituals that helped reproduce the image of the corporation as the ultimate source of all authority. In October 1988, Roger Smith, then the chief executive officer, sponsored a very different kind of top management conference. In the past, senior executive forums were "exercises in tedium or terror" in which "managers would be seated in rows to listen while GM leadership gave speech after speech."[4] But at this conference, stimulated in part by a sense that the company was facing a crisis, managers from different levels of the organization worked together for the first time in smaller groups on particular "breakthrough" issues. Leadership, one observer noted, "was everyone in the room."

No doubt, many of the managers at the aforementioned meeting felt cautious about touching on difficult topics. Nor can we dismiss the possibility that GM's senior management, sensing that its legitimacy was slipping, used this new conference design to placate the discontented. But, in line with the argument developed here, the meeting ritual had essentially changed; the conference design did help people bring up new or once-taboo ideas, and managers were no longer overwhelmed by the image of an indivisible and inaccessible center of authority. The image of a central and distant power gave way to an image of many centers of power based on the personal authority participants mobilized to help answer novel questions. This is another reasons why I call such a development post-modern. Power, as scholars of post-modernism would say, was "deconstructed"; it entered into the network of personal authority rather than staying concentrated at the organizational center.

Reconstructing Organizations

The modern enterprise did not emerge without conflict and difficulty. General Motors nearly collapsed as a result of the buccaneering of its founder, Will Durant, before he was deposed in 1920. Ford almost failed in the late 1930s; it survived because Henry Ford II substituted a rational system of management for the arbitrary exercise of power his grandfather had encouraged. Because the corporation centralized so much power in a few individuals, it was always at risk of devouring itself from within.

Alfred P. Sloan had the genius to recognize that, in an organization dependent on both power and predictability, corporate leaders had to rationalize the organization's process. A corporation focused

4. Maryann Keller, *Rude Awakening* (Harper, 1989), p. 238.

on a single leader could not sustain itself, however charismatic or terrifying the leader might be. It had to become more impersonal to protect itself from the exercise of arbitrary power. Sloan and succeeding executives introduced personnel systems and financial control systems to regulate the relationships between bosses and subordinates and between the employee and the company. They created a system of governance by balancing the power of headquarters and divisions. Unions helped solidify this system of administration by regulating the power dynamics between supervisors and frontline workers. Indeed, Sloan's greatest limitation as an executive was his failure to recognize that workers on the factory floor had to be part of his new system of regulation and control.[5]

While the modern enterprise reduced the exercise of arbitrary power, it also developed in its wake a climate of suppression and conformity—what Weber called the "iron cage" of bureaucracy. The executive suite on the fourteenth floor of the General Motors building typified this climate in the extreme: "The first thing you notice is the deafening silence. There are no stray laughs drifting down the long hallway. No bustling workers racing by with reams of paper. No heated voices raised. As you walk along the corridor you might not see anyone at all. Everyone on the floor . . . works behind closed doors." [6]

The modern enterprise thus offered employees a psychological deal with the devil: in exchange for both predictability and protection from arbitrary decisions, they were asked to withdraw their psychological presence[7] from work. This was the sense in which the white-collar worker, the managerial employee of the twentieth century, was "alienated."

However, because individuals gained as well as lost something in this system of administration, they will not relinquish easily the attitudes they have inherited from it. Managers once kept at a social distance from senior executives (increasing, in turn, their striving to join them) may feel skeptical, even cynical, when an executive asks

5. Abraham Zaleznik, "The Mythological Structure of Organizations and its Impact," in *The Psychodynamics of Organizations*, ed. L. Hirschhorn and C. Barnett (Temple University Press, 1993).

6. *Rude Awakening*, p. 17.

7. The concept of psychological presence has been developed by William Kahn. See "To Be Fully There," *Human Relations* 45 (1992), no. 4: 321–349.

them to participate in strategic decisions. They may wonder what he has up his sleeve. Similarly, factory managers who imagine that they are being heroes when they announce that they have "empowered employees" are disappointed, even embittered, when the troops do not thank them for this wonderful opportunity. Employees and executives are also disappointed when the post-modern enterprise does not grant them complete autonomy. An engineer asked to be creative and entrepreneurial is flabbergasted when his or her terrific idea for a new machine is not funded: "I've been betrayed," the engineer thinks, not acknowledging that as individuals become more creative, they also compete more with others for scarce resources. The transition to the post-modern enterprise is thus filled with difficulties and contradictions.

Example: An Electronics Factory

Consider the predicament faced by the senior managers of an electronics factory.[8] Eager to empower their workers, they had inadvertently exposed first-line supervisors to derision. Workers participating in a quality-improvement seminar at the factory attacked supervisors for what appeared to be their arbitrary practices. Supervisors, feeling unjustly accused and scapegoated, were demoralized. The human resources manager of the plant approached my consulting firm: Could we conduct some seminars for the supervisors? Could we help them redefine their own roles as workers took on more responsibility?

In conjunction with supervisors and managers, we developed a seminar program based on current situations. The three-day seminar was conducted four different times. In each seminar we met alone with the supervisors for the first two days, and then with senior management and the supervisors together on the last day.

At the end of the second day of the fourth and last seminar, the supervisors grew tense. Asked to report to senior management on their ideas for changing plant practices, they worried that their thinking might not be respected. The senior managers appeared interested and responsive—yet, surprisingly, the supervisors still felt

8. For a more detailed development of this case see Larry Hirschhorn and Thomas Gilmore, "The Psychodynamics of Cultural Change," in *The Psychodynamics of Organizations*, ed. Hirschhorn and Barnett.

disappointed. They mistrusted their managers' apparent acquiescence. The managers, they thought, were withholding thoughts and feelings so as to "get through" the seminar. Their meeting lacked the expected drama. It was as if the supervisors were asking "Is this all there is?"

Indeed, this anxiety was partly confirmed at the end of the seminar. The plant manager, clearly pleased with his experience, told the assembled group of senior managers and supervisors that he was no longer their commander but rather their cheerleader. He would stand on the sidelines as supervisors developed new styles of leadership. The supervisors had to wonder, however, who would hold a cheerleader accountable for the plant's performance. Indeed, the plant manager's statement smacked of abdication.

This vignette highlights some of the difficulties individuals in organizations face when senior managers try to create a more open and participative culture. The workers, while claiming to be grateful, were also angry. Facing persons in authority who for the first time wanted to know what they as a group thought, they dumped on their supervisors. Similarly, the supervisors were suspicious. They had worked within a tight chain of command for so many years that they could not believe that they might collaborate in a collegial way with their bosses. Finally, the plant manager sidestepped the problem of collaborating with the men and women he had once commanded by telling them he would be their cheerleader.

This book characterizes many variations on the preceding story. It illuminates what happens to us and to our relatedness with others at work as we make the transition from the modern to the post-modern enterprise. Chapter 1 shows how all these stories are anchored ultimately in what I call "the dilemmas of openness"—of making oneself open and vulnerable to the ideas, thoughts, and feelings of others. As individuals become more psychologically present to one another and to authority figures, they also become more psychologically open and potentially vulnerable. They risk feeling ashamed when they broach a novel idea or express a spontaneous feeling. At the root of the post-modern enterprise lies a new "culture of openness" that promises great gains for individual and organizational performance but also threatens to exact great costs from individual leaders and followers. In chapter 1, I explore the meaning of a culture of openness by considering what we mean by the self in a postmodern age.

For previous publications of case material discussed herein, see the following: "Hierarchy versus Bureaucracy: The Case of the Nuclear Reactor," in Karlene H. Roberts, *New Challenges to Understanding Organizations* (Macmillan, 1993); "Organizational Change and Adult Learning," in *What Makes Workers Learn*, ed. D. Hirsch and D. Wagner (Hampton, 1995); "Organized Feelings toward Authority: A Case Study of Reflective Action," in *The Reflective Turn*, ed. D. Schon (Teachers College Press, 1990); "The Psychodynamics of Safety," in *The Psychodynamics of Organizations*, ed. L. Hirschhorn and C. Barnett (Temple University Press, 1993).

1

The Self, Modern and Post-Modern

The modern sensibility highlighted individualism—the belief that one could shape one's future according to one's own wishes and impulses. But the modern sensibility was also characterized by the idea of "character," a core of being that stamped each person as unique. In the nineteenth century, the cultural conception of character—the self—became extremely important in shaping the individual's conception of his or her life's task. Young religious believers went through a ritual of "conversion" in which they resolved doubt and fixed character. "Conversion," Joseph Kett notes, "was linked to identity, it involved the selection of some aspects of one's personality at the expense of others."[1] Physicians argued that a young man could strengthen his character by resisting the temptation to masturbate. Educators and philosophers asserted that a young man who pursued an interest single-mindedly would succeed. Herbert Croly notes that "a man achieves individual distinction, not by the enterprise and vigor with which he accumulates money, but by the zeal and skill with which he pursues an exclusive interest. . . . It becomes exclusive for the individual who adopts it, because of the single-minded and disinterested manner in which it is pursued."[2] This conception of character gave rise to the modern conception of the masculine ideal: a man who suppresses doubt and ambivalence, is single-minded in the pursuit of his goals, and has an unshakable commitment to his own character.

The post-modern enterprise is built upon a different conception: that of an individual who uses doubt as a springboard for learning

1. Joseph Kett, *Rites of Passage* (Basic Books, 1977), p. 81.

2. Herbert Croly, *The Promise of American Life* (Harvard University Press, 1965), pp. 411–412

and exposes his or her inner character to the feelings that others stimulate. We call such an individual "open" or "vulnerable" in the sense that he or she is open to being influenced deeply by ongoing experience—i.e., the person learns from experience. Character is not fixed but instead unfolds over the adult life course. Similarly, we say that the post-modern organization sustains a "culture of being open to others"—in shorthand, a "culture of openness."

This culture of openness poses psychological risks, for in being open and therefore vulnerable individuals risk feeling ashamed. For example, in the past, management meetings at the electronics factory described in the introductory chapter were organized as performances. Individuals prepared for a meeting so that it could go off without a hitch, so that no real learning or discovery took place. This paradigm for meetings certainly helped all the members contain their anxiety—there would be no surprises; individuals who had performed badly could read the "signal" of the bosses' displeasure without being shamed in public; and the leader, fully in control, could protect his self-image as highly competent, if not invulnerable. The downside of this paradigm is that managers could not meet to do creative work together. Feeling suppressed by the format but also understanding the larger risks the organization faced, people rushed out of the meeting at breaks to gossip about who was on top and on bottom today, who was scoring points, and who was losing credibility. The gossip relieved their anxiety and returned to them a sense of participating, at least in the "dirt" of the organization, at the cost of failing to contribute to substantive discussions and decisions.

But if senior managers decide to hold more authentic and thoughtful meetings, they and the participants must take risks. Members have to ask: "If I think my own idea is a good one, but others think I am stupid, will they think less of me, or appreciate me for the courage I showed in 'stepping out of the box'?" The senior manager has to ask: "If I ask questions that suggest I don't know what I am talking about, will I lose the respect of my followers, or will they welcome my openness and my invitation to them to help me?" The post-modern organization requires that individuals at all levels make themselves more open to one another—how else can it draw on the individual creativity of all its members?—but faces the stark reality that people don't wish to look incompetent or feel ashamed.

The following examples and vignettes let us explore the tensions people face as they make this transition, unawares, from the culture of the modern to the culture of the post-modern enterprise.

The Leader as Person: The Need for Vulnerability

I first met Frank, a vice-president of a large division in a pharmaceutical company, while he was attending an executive education program at a local business school. We met to assess whether I could help him as he developed his own leadership abilities. He began by sketching his company's various divisions on a flip chart, then indicated how much revenue each division generated. I was struck by his control of the facts and by how easily he described the company's organization. He seemed comfortable discussing the billions of dollars generated by the different divisions and describing management's resource-allocation decisions. This man seemed to be "in charge."

As Frank continued, however, I became increasingly confused about his role. When he finally identified his position—senior executive of a division within a subsidiary—I realized that his ease of presentation had led me to believe that he was much closer in rank to the company's most senior executives than he actually was. Moreover, I realized that he had never mentioned his own subordinates, the people he worked with everyday. I began to suspect that I was discovering a fantasy he had about himself: that he worked only with numbers and dollars and was a grand strategist collaborating with the company's top management.

Hoping to gain more insight, I stopped Frank in the middle of his story and asked him to tell me about the people he worked with. To my surprise, he sat down as if deflated and began to describe the confusion he felt in leading his own team. Senior management had dramatically restructured the company in the last five years and now required the divisions to produce more profit, greater revenues, and higher-quality products, but with fewer people and greater attention to productivity and safety. The company had sponsored many programs to improve effectiveness in areas such as quality, safety, and work simplification, and these programs had greatly complicated the task of managing the activities of Frank's division.

In addition, following the example of other division vice-presidents and responding to pressure from his own team, Frank had started a "visioning process," working with those reporting directly to him and some of their subordinates to produce a vision for his division. Yet he felt uncertain about the value of this activity. He asked me what I thought of vision statements: Could they be written without being linked to a business plan? Had he been right to "yield" to his subordinates' pressure to write such a statement? If the statement affirmed employees' rights to a better quality of work life, would he be "shooting himself in the foot"? After several years of cutbacks, his employees could only feel overworked and exploited, and what could he do about that?

Listening to Frank, I understood that his subordinates were painful reminders of the confusion he faced in linking all these corporate programs and objectives to the day-to-day work of his division. Feeling confused themselves, his subordinates wanted a vision, but Frank was not sure he could give them one. Perhaps he could not lead them, he felt. It now became clear why I had overestimated Frank's position at first: He was feeling uncertain of his own role. By appearing to be more important than he was, he was not simply trying to impress me. Rather, he was projecting a defensive fantasy that made him feel more in control of his situation than he actually was. In doing so, however, Frank not only distanced himself from me; he also distanced himself psychologically from the very people on whom he had to depend in order to do his work successfully. To break out of this vicious circle, Frank needed to affirm his confusion—his vulnerability—and see it as a starting point for his development rather than as a signal of defeat.

Frank, I suggest, was facing the difficulties of leading in a postmodern organization. The individual leader needs talent and imagination but today cannot grasp the complexities of the social field alone. The leader needs subordinates. This requirement challenges leaders' sophistication and maturity. All leaders must have sufficient self-regard to cope with the disappointments ambition inevitably produces. Their "narcissism" helps them sacrifice current pleasures for the sake of an ideal image of their lives while protecting them from the psychological damage competitors want to inflict. Today's leaders must also acknowledge their dependence on others and become open to the others' strengths and weaknesses so they can get the help they need. Therefore, they face the complex task of identifying with their ambitions and their limitations simultaneously. They must step beyond their formal roles and present themselves to their subordinates as human beings having not just strengths but also limits and uncertainties.

The Leader as Role: The Need for Organizational Authority

Being open to subordinates requires a leader to reveal more of his or her "personhood." One cannot hide behind the role of leader; instead, one must bring more of one's passions, fears, and values to it. Yet the leadership role cannot be ignored. A leader can neither pretend to be "just one person talking to another" nor act as if differences in power and authority between him and his subordinates are negligible. The post-modern enterprise is still a performance organization, It must allocate scarce human and material resources to specific goals. How can a leader strike this balance between being open and vulnerable and taking charge? In the following example we see how one leader failed to strike this balance and instead substituted seductiveness for openness.

Harry, the senior partner of a public relations firm, was an enormously charming man who was well liked by his associates. Several of the women in particular felt comfortable remonstrating with him; for example, at times they told him not to talk for other women at the firm's meetings and to let associates finish their sentences. I felt drawn to the firm's family atmosphere and the camaraderie that encouraged humor and spontaneity.

Yet, as I learned at a two-day retreat, this informality was matched by a feeling that secrets and cabals shaped much of the firm's development. For example, a year earlier the firm's three principals had nominated two associates to the partnership, but neither had been able to generate business and both had left the firm before the retreat. The remaining associates were enraged. Why had these two people been made partners? What criteria had been used? Why had these decisions seemingly been made behind closed doors? Why did the firm have no public criteria for advancement? Why did the partners' decision making often seem arbitrary? The firm's promotion policy was the paramount subject during the retreat. In effect, because the partners—particularly Harry—related to the firm as if it were their family, they also treated it as their private domain. Harry's personable style and warmth deprived the firm of the *qualities of an organization*—the roles, rules, and procedures that help people feel secure. Indeed, because it lacked organization, the firm was not growing as rapidly as it could. Although they were experts in public relations, the partners were unable and unwilling to actually shape a marketing plan and a process that could discipline the work of all the firm's members. Ultimately, the firm suffered from Harry's excessive personalism and his inability to take on a more formal role.

In a post-modern milieu, a leader cannot use his or her role to hide uncertainty and vulnerability. However, a leader who denies the salience of his formal role and the differences between himself and his subordinates can create a climate of uncertainty and insecurity. In short: a leader can lean too much toward the *role* or too much toward the *person*. Frank hid behind his role as leader to such an extent that he projected the image of a leader with more power than he actually had while his subordinates clamored for collaboration (i.e., the "visioning process"). Harry set up a false intimacy that mimicked collaboration but in fact barred his followers from participating in crucial discussions and decisions. His followers were trapped in the dynamics of feeling close to him and were denied the organizational structure that a leader must provide.

Followers

Followers too have responsibilities. If their leader asks for help, can they respond? What are the experiences and anxieties of followers?

Consider the following vignette: A co-consultant and I were working with a superintendent of schools and his principals on the challenge of decentralizing the governance of their school district. We first met with the principals and asked them to develop questions for the superintendent about "site-based" (i.e., school-building-based) management. The questions were sensible and conveyed the principals' anxieties. Most important, the principals wanted to know how the superintendent would evaluate their performance in this new system of governance and what level of confusion in school buildings he would tolerate.

The superintendent (Greg) then joined the meeting. As Greg examined the list of questions and talked with the principals, it soon became obvious that he had no clear answers. He was not sure how his role and theirs would be shaped by the politics of the board of education. He noted that, with taxpayers demanding objective measures of teacher performance, the entire evaluation system could be revised. He seemed comfortable with his own uncertainty, periodically saying: "I don't know. I'm thinking out loud here." He did, however, emphasize that the principal of a school, while promoting teachers' participation, should have control over basics such as bus schedules, supplies, and the budget. He argued that without these basics in place, teacher participation would never work.

Curiously, when Greg was present the principals seemed tongue-tied and their conversation was stiff. After Greg left and the principals examined their encounter with him, they were genuinely puzzled by their own passivity. They felt certain, however, that Greg had warned them, in an almost punishing way, to get control of the basic management tasks in their buildings. I asked the principals: "Did you feel that Greg was punishing you just now?" Several said that indeed he was. I suggested that Greg's thinking, although not completely coherent, was certainly complex and could not be reduced to a few simple injunctions or remonstrations. I also said that Greg was exploring difficult issues in the same way they were.

What was going on? The principals were clearly anxious about their ability to function in a decentralized setting. Perhaps they were passive because they had hoped Greg would tell them how to function in this new setting and assure them, despite their confusion, that they were indeed good managers. When he did not meet their needs for dependence, when he did not give them answers, they were not able to talk directly with him. Adults who assume professional roles expect to feel competent. When they feel incompetent—as when the principals were tongue-tied—they feel ashamed. This suggests that the principals interpreted their inarticulateness as a sign that they were bad managers.

This interpretation suggests why, when Greg suggested that a participative climate could develop only in a setting where the basics were secured, the principals considered it a reproach—a statement that they were bad building managers. In short, when their leader revealed his confusion as well as his willingness to collaborate with his subordinates, this frightened the principals. Consequently, they grew passive and tongue-tied, and instead of regarding Greg as open they felt that he was punishing their perceived incompetence.

Clearly, the prospect of decentralized decision making in the schools (i.e., site-based management) made the principals feel insecure and anxious. Indeed, while Greg was being shown the flip chart with their questions, one principal (Fred) whispered frequently to a colleague on his right, like a schoolboy, but never contributed to the group discussion. He then stood up, walked to the flip chart, and changed the word "our" to "my" in the question "How will this program affect our evaluations?" At first, I was struck by Fred's willingness to expose his anxiety. Yet his schoolboy whispering seemed inconsistent with courage. I then hypothesized that when he had changed the word on the chart he had acted not as an adult taking a risk but as a dependent child who simply wanted protection. Concerned primarily about his performance, he was not ready to collaborate with Greg. Consequently, while other principals expressed their anxiety through silence, Fred expressed his through whispering, defying Greg as a child might defy a teacher and thus actually giving expression to his dependence.

Example: The Electronics Factory Again

Recall the electronics factory mentioned in the introductory chapter. At the end of the second seminar, the plant manager and his assistant (the director for development and quality, who typically attended the last session of the seminar) were prevented by schedule conflicts from joining the supervisors in the final hours of their work together. I and the other two members of my consulting team grew nervous. We were uncertain how we could end the seminar. With what authority could we bring it to a close, and what themes or issues should we emphasize? I suggested to the leader of the consulting team (Vincent) that at the seminar's end we three consultants go to the front of the seminar room and ask for final reflections and thoughts on the work that had been done. He agreed. Five minutes before the scheduled time for ending the seminar, one supervisor called out "Let's thank the consultants" and everyone clapped. Vincent, who was standing in front, called me and the third member of our team to the front of the room, and we sat down facing the supervisors. Following the plan, Vincent then asked if anyone wanted to say something to "close out or complete some unfinished work." Silence followed and anxiety grew. No one felt authorized to speak. We waited in silence, facing the supervisors. After a minute or two, one supervisor broke the silence by turning to Vincent and asking him, as if he were on a television talk show, what he thought about the state of the American economy. Vincent answered briefly; again silence followed. I stood up, noted that I simply wanted to make contact with the group and say goodbye, and then sat down. More silence followed. Vincent closed the meeting, and the supervisors fled the room as if we had introduced some poison into the air.

I have never had such an intense and unexpected feeling of alienation, of being suddenly without a connection to anyone. What had happened? Anxious to find a structure for closing out the seminar and feeling let down by the absence of the two chief executives, we had created the core properties of an authority boundary. That is, by going to the front of the room and facing the group, we had drawn an invisible yet palpable line between us and the supervisors. We had assumed the authority role typically taken by top managers of the plant. We had, therefore, evoked the plant's primary struggle: Can leaders and followers communicate across the authority divide?

What happens when leaders expose themselves in the way we did? What do followers do when their leaders' dependence on them for action, thinking, and attention is made so transparent? How do followers deal with leaders who abdicate—who do not show up for the final moments of an important event? What happens to the resulting disappointment; how is it expressed? Finally, in taking the places of the plant manager and his assistant, were we denying our dependence on them? Had we not refused to recognize that without them we could not possibly end the event in satisfactory way? We were helpless but could not admit it.

We feel alienated when we seek contact and are not just turned away, but when the fact of our seeking contact is itself turned away—denied. We are ashamed for having revealed our unmet need for contact. I propose that this shame—this exposure and the resulting feelings of alienation—creates the hidden psychological injuries of the post-modern organization.

The Plan of the Book

Using a series of case studies, this book explores the challenges of
openness that leaders and followers confront as they build and work
in the post-modern organization. It is based on the following propositions, which will be explored throughout:

• Individuals in organizations face two sources of vulnerability. Not
only must they take the risk of being open to one another, but everyone in the organization is vulnerable to the risks the enterprise faces
as a whole. New markets, competitors, technologies, and stakeholders threaten to undermine the strategies leaders have traditionally
used to guide the enterprise. This challenge is experienced by employees at all levels: the supervisors who see inventory accumulate
as sales falls, the salespeople who note that returns are growing, the
controller who monitors the growth of short-term debt, the CEO who
calculates that the cost of acquiring new customers is rising.
Although no single employee has a complete picture of the risks facing the enterprise, all are aware of these dents in the system. These
symptoms of decline cannot be hidden; everyone feels vulnerable to
them.

• If leaders and followers are not prepared for such a setting, they
will cope inappropriately by imagining that the sources of danger lie
within the organization rather than outside it. Another division,
one's peers, one's subordinates, or one's bosses become seen as the
major threats to one's position, security, and identity. Alternatively,
the external threat is denied and particular leaders or projects are
idealized. Hope that is based on a realistic assessment of risk is displaced by a fantasy that the risks have already been overcome.

• Authority relationships fuel the psychological transformation of
outside risks into inside threats. Threat and risk always mobilize our
fantasies about our relationships with authority figures and their rep-
resentation in rules, procedures, schedules, and divisional boundaries. When we are facing threats, our forgotten feelings of
dependence on parents and teachers resurface. Will they protect us,
harm us, divide us? These feelings and fantasies can *organize* our attempts to cope with current risks and threats. For example, some followers may imagine that they, in contrast to others, are protected
from a threat because they have a special relationship with a leader.
Leaders may abdicate their authority and blame followers for the failure of the enterprise. Followers may hate a leader while denying that
the leader's skills are protecting and developing the organization.

• As the market becomes more turbulent, we must not let these psychological processes exert too great a pull on our thinking and acting,

for doing so threatens the work of the enterprise. Instead, we must develop a culture of openness in which leaders, followers, and peers make themselves vulnerable to one another as a precondition for confronting the external challenges they face. They must acknowledge how each has contributed to the organization's successes and failures while mobilizing each person's strengths and limiting the negative effect of each person's weakness.

• Thus, to create a culture of openness, organizations must first and foremost build new relationships to authority. Leaders must make themselves more vulnerable to their peers and their subordinates. They must risk their *apparent authority* (the authority that announces that they are in charge) in the interest of deepening their *substantive authority* (the authority they gain from leading a successful team performance). Followers, for their part, must overcome both their excessive dependence on authority and their blanket hostility to it. In both challenging and accepting authority, one learns to *lead as a follower.*

• When leaders and followers cannot develop these new authority relationships, they suppress their genuine needs for help from their peers and from one another. Seeking to protect themselves by limiting their vulnerability, they unwittingly create psychologically covert processes that alienate them from others and from the organization's real work—and the real work suffers.

• As the post-modern organization becomes more vulnerable in its market, its leaders and followers must become more vulnerable to one another if the enterprise is to succeed. Whereas in the past enterprise leaders increased their control in the market by controlling their subordinates, today enterprise leaders must release their own subordinates to regain such control in their market.

• Building the post-modern enterprise is thus like walking across a trapeze. Facing greater market risks, the enterprise asks its employees be more open, more vulnerable to one another. But in becoming more vulnerable, people compound their sense of risk. They are threatened from without and within. If this sense of risk becomes too strong, people will withdraw from their roles; they will be psychologically absent. Having become absent, they can no longer retreat to their previous roles, which are now dysfunctional. Thus the stage is set for a more primitive psychology. Individuals question their own competence and their ability to act autonomously. In consequence, just when they need to build a more sophisticated psychological culture, they inadvertently create a more primitive one.

• The forces for such regression are strengthened by job and career loss. In the transition to a post-industrial society, anxiety about their jobs leads individuals to withhold information, know-how, and simple helpfulness from one another. They experience their own vulnerability more than the organization's vulnerability. The stage is set for a new dialectic between a new and more adaptive psychology of openness and an increasingly primitive search for invulnerability.

The Approach

This book's argument is made through the presentation of case studies and vignettes, all of which derive from my own experience as a consultant. The purpose of a case study is to explore the psychological terrain people are likely to encounter as they cross the divide between the modern and the post-modern enterprise. The discussion of each case is based on the psychodynamics of individuals and groups in organizations—a frame of reference that is itself based on applied psychoanalysis. Applied psychoanalysis refers to the use of such psychoanalytic ideas as "the unconscious," "projection," "defenses," and "fantasies."[3]

As the expression goes, when the water level falls the rocks are exposed. In this book the rocks are exposed in chapters 2–5. Over several centuries we have learned how to harness and suppress our natures to the modern enterprise. But we are now losing this balance of expression and suppression. Fundamental human feelings which we once knew how to sublimate or suppress through our working activity—passion, ambition, insecurity, dependence—are now left unchannelled. Unless we learn to re-integrate them into the post-modern enterprise in a way that supports both the fullness of the enterprise and the fullness of these feelings, we will regress both emotionally and in terms of our performance.

The case studies in chapters 2–5 are built upon the following sequence of arguments: First, I identify a key feeling or state of mind associated with organizational life, such as "dependency," "the technocratic mind," or the "hero fantasy." Second, I explore how this feeling or state of mind is enacted in the case presented. Then I ask how this feeling or state of mind if, unmodified and left underdeveloped, can leads to organizational and personal regression.

3. For a full explication of these ideas see my book *The Workplace Within* (MIT Press, 1990).

Finally, I describe how this feeling could be developed—made more sophisticated—so that people could use it to perform more effectively in the post-modern enterprise.

Chapters 2–5 are not arranged in a logical order. Rather, each represents an independent probe into the organizational psychodynamics of the transition period. One might think of this portion of the book as a spoked wheel, with each spoke representing one particular manifestation of the theme of openness. In chapter 2 I show how individuals cope with their feelings of dependence on leaders, and how their methods of coping may limit their felt and actual competence. In chapter 3 I highlight how the technocratic mind can inhibit the passion leaders need to feel and demonstrate if they are to engage their followers in complicated strategic tasks. In chapter 4 I show what happens when leaders facing significant risks to their enterprise abdicate their leadership roles. In chapter 5 I point out how an organizational culture of heroism helps people deny the threats they face while also creating villains who come to represent these threats.

In chapters 6 and 7 I return to the theme of the post-modern sensibility. Having shown in chapters 2–5 how the post-modern enterprise is built upon a new organizational psychodynamics, I argue in chapter 6 that these dynamics are linked to a new and broader "cultural sensibility"—a new way of experiencing our inner selves and their relationship to others' inner selves. Just as the Reformation and its cultural aftereffects fostered the creation of the modern enterprise, this new sensibility, if understood and developed, can help us develop the post-modern enterprise. However, just as an organization can regress as it "crosses the post-modern divide,"[4] our culture can also regress, so that the new sensibility stands only as a foil for other, more destructive cultural tendencies.

In chapter 7, looking at the case of a strategy consulting firm, I show how this wider sensibility can help leaders and followers develop a more intense and more "feelingful" group life together. The concluding chapter assesses some of the major political and economic impediments we face in building the post-modern enterprise

4. See Albert Borgmann, *Crossing the Postmodern Divide* (University of Chicago Press, 1992).

Summary

The post-modern enterprise is shaped both by the new technologies of information and communication and by the new culture of openness. The new technologies place great emphasis on employees' ability to act autonomously, to make decisions in the face of significant uncertainty, and to participate in the strategic decisions enterprise leaders make. The new openness, where it develops and flourishes, can help people work in such a setting. It creates enough psychological safety so that people will risk being more psychologically present and will use their thoughts and feelings to create new ideas and discover new solutions.

Individuals are at this nexus between culture and technology. They alone decide how spontaneous they can be, how much they can reveal, how many of their own errors they can accept, to what extent they can tolerate the scrutiny of others, and how much public risk they wish to shoulder. We will not be able to navigate the transition between the modern and the post-modern enterprise unless we understand how the psychology of individuals and groups—their "psychodynamics"—will shape and be shaped by the post-modern enterprise. The book reports on the struggles taking place on this terrain.

2

Dependency

In organizational and social life we depend on the skills of those who are superior to us in talent to solve hard problems, to invent concepts, systems and products we can use fruitfully, and to make difficult judgments that entail hurting some people while protecting others (e.g., sending soldiers to war).

But adults are uneasy with their feelings of dependence. They feel vulnerable to those who have power and who may act arbitrarily and injure them. Adults are often ashamed of their dependence. For example, it is difficult for adults to become students again, because they resent submitting to instructors as they did when they were children.

I had a vivid experience of this process when consulting with the nursing department of a large hospital. The six-person top team of the nursing department had established a "congress" in which supervisory nurses were to determine department policy by deliberating and coming to a consensus on policy questions. The congress failed. Although the elected executive committee would identify tasks forces to consider particular issues and make recommendations to the congress, members of the congress could not agree to accept or reject the task force's recommendations. Most members felt that the congress's purpose and functioning should be substantially modified. Yet when the top team considered abolishing the congress or substantially modifying its mandate, a minority of the congress's members complained. They were embarrassed that, despite their evident competence (they were all supervisors and managers), they had to relinquish their autonomy because they had failed to govern themselves.

Similarly, consider the following example: I once consulted to a retreat of the executive team of the research and development division of a chemical company. The division's vice-president, a brilliant organizer, exercised considerable control over the work of a number of individuals. He created and sustained a highly disciplined process of screening large numbers of compounds for potentially useful chemicals. At the retreat he was also abusive and domineering, silencing everyone not by shouting but by overtalking while making intelligent and thoughtful comments on organizational issues. While fearful of him, most scientist-managers responded by trying to please him. They acted seductively, laughed at his jokes, cajoled him, joined him for meals so he might regale them with stories. Indeed, I found that at meals he created a convivial feeling. Subordinates did not wish to cross him, but by behaving seductively they could develop the fantasy that they could in fact control him. By reinforcing his fantasy as the patriarch of a close-knit family, they could "get under his skin" and thus reduce their dependence on him. Fearful and ashamed to be so dominated, they could develop a compensatory culture that restored to them a sense of control while also creating a climate of informality.

As these episodes suggest, dependency can provoke feelings of shame and fear. These feelings can drive the feeling of dependence underground so that it is expressed indirectly—for example, in resentment, childish rebelliousness (e.g., stealing office supplies), or seductiveness. However, in denying our dependence on others and our consequent vulnerability to decisions we don't control we take two risks. First, we make it difficult for genuinely talented people to help us. Second, in developing compensatory fantasies, as the executives of the aforementioned R&D organization did, we don't challenge the talented professionals or leaders around us when they make mistakes. Why challenge them when we imagine that we have subtler ways of controlling them?

The Modern Organization

The modern organization, when it functioned well, contained the impact of these potentially destabilizing feelings by *depersonalizing* dependence. Individuals experienced dominance and submission as artifacts of their role relationships. They might, consequently, take a "political" view of their situation (e.g., that they were participating in the drama of "labor versus capital"), or they might develop a moral or normative stance (e.g., "one should obey ones superiors"). Similarly, factory supervisors who disciplined workers could protect themselves from feelings of guilt and anxiety by ascribing their harshness to the roles they occupied. While never completely resolving the tension between person and role, the modern organization, by favoring the role, created a paradoxically helpful climate of depersonalization.

The post-modern organization disrupts this climate. As we have seen, individuals increasingly rely on their person rather than their role to find their authority for making decisions. But personalization challenges us. In the past, inherited hierarchies, the class system, and a common moral code all protected us from the conflicting feelings that genuine dependence created. In the post-modern era, feelings of dependence masquerading in such acts as psychological seduction and rebellion can, once these feelings are exposed, undermine authority relationships.

In this chapter I explore the vicissitudes of dependency. I show how the members of an international aid organization with roots in the culture of 1960s were burdened by their own informality. By paying little attention to roles, they became too dependent on their valued leader, losing in the process their own sense of competence. Personalization, paradoxically, reinforced dependence.

Example: International Help

International Help, an agency founded by Peace Corps veterans in the mid 1970s, had a central staff of about 25 and numerous field workers. It funded and directed projects in Third World countries through which poor people obtained housing, education, and food. Program staffers at the central office created these projects, obtained funding for them, recruited field staffers to manage them, and monitored their progress at a distance for the duration of the project. The work was rewarding but frequently difficult, since members of the central staff, while feeling accountable for field programs, often had little control over field staffers' activities.

The Leader's Dominance

I first entered International Help when Sam, a program director, asked me to meet with Carol, about 55 years old and the agency's longtime executive director. Carol, Sam felt, was overloaded and had become nearly indispensable to the organization. Her staffers valued her leadership and professional competence highly and went to her for advice on all matters of program development. Carol, in turn, exercised complete control over the programs. She reviewed all grant proposals, edited all outgoing documents, and kept abreast of the field work.

Although the agency was ostensibly organized into divisions, with each program director responsible for a particular region of the world, Carol was in charge of all key program decisions. The program directors functioned more as staff assistants to her than as directors. For example, at their weekly meetings with Carol they did little but have their own staffs report directly to Carol on the latest field developments. Far from organizing the mass of details from the field and presenting important issues to Carol, the program directors functioned as administrators. They assumed no executive authority and felt no responsibility for developing programmatic overviews of their respective regions. Thus, while nominally in charge of their regions, they functioned as colleagues to their subordinates and as staff assistants to Carol. There was no real chain of command.

One manager expressed this feeling of dependence and lack of authority quite poignantly. At a group meeting of program managers he noted that when Carol had last been away on a trip he had felt stymied and had not known what to do in several program areas for which he was responsible. This puzzled him, he said: "I feel like a competent professional, like an adult. Why can't I act in Carol's absence?" I suggested that perhaps he felt that Carol psychologically owned part of his job, that it was not entirely his. He smiled and nodded his head strongly.

Issues Presented by the Program Staff

At my first meeting with Carol and Sam, Carol acknowledged the potential burden she faced: the organization, successful in raising funds and expanding its programs, had become too large for her to manage. While open to considering changes, she was skeptical that after all these years she and I, along with her program staff, could develop new ways of working. Nonetheless, she was willing to try, and she agreed that I should begin by interviewing her staff.

My interviews with the program staff highlighted some of the structural issues that led Carol to manage the organization in such detail. Managing complex service programs from afar in often politically volatile settings created substantial risks for International Help. Field staffers might find it difficult to implement programs in the form promised to funders, and central staffers worried that field staffers might be co-opted by local political groups or elites and find themselves involved in political struggles. The program staffers felt that Carol had the experience, capacity, and knowledge to take in an enormous amount of detail and felt far more comfortable letting her make the critical and ongoing program decisions than doing it themselves. Nonetheless, all agreed that Carol was in danger of taking on too much work. She spent nearly three working months a year in meetings, met with all the organization's funders and political supporters, wrote proposals, and (as already mentioned) reviewed and edited all written work and correspondence.

The Dynamics of Dependence

I was puzzled that a not-for-profit organization whose culture and history were rooted in the spirit of the early Peace Corps and the social values of the 1960s could tolerate such tight control by one person. I suspected that, in part, Carol's sheer competence, her commitment to her work, the political values that shaped that work, and the quiet and sustained quality of her concentration and attention enabled people to submit to her judgment and authority unequivocally. However, I now believe that the relationships between Carol and the members of her staff were partly shaped by the psychodynamics of dependence and vulnerability.

One vignette is striking here. When I first met Carol and Sam, they both emphasized the difficulty everyone was having with Bill, who had been brought in about half a year before to assist Carol. People felt that Bill was trying to act too much like a deputy, trying to supervise the programs by examining and correcting grants and reviewing field correspondence. As they spoke at length about the many problems he was causing, I imagined that Bill might be obstructing Carol's increasing willingness to delegate some authority. Before meeting him, I expected him to be a willful, strong-minded person intent on concentrating power in his role.

Nothing could have been farther from the truth. Bill was a gentle and unassuming person, scholarly in demeanor, who felt hurt and confused by people's suspicion of him and by the difficulty he faced in carving out a role. He thought he had been hired to relieve Carol of some of her work, as it had been explained to him by board members; however, he told me he had no desire to be Carol's deputy if she didn't want one. Most of all, he wanted some clarification of his role and some real tasks so that he could contribute to International Help's mission while enjoying his work. I was convinced by his manner and moved by his genuine pain. Why had Carol and Sam created an image of Bill as the "bad guy"?

I hypothesized that people tolerated Carol's overwhelming dominance because each program manager or staffer imagined or hoped that he or she had a special relationship with Carol. Since each person, regardless of formal title, had direct access to Carol who supervised them all directly, each of them did in fact have the privilege of working directly with her. However, I imagined that many an individual fantasized that he or she had the *most* special relationship to with her. For example, Sam confidently told me that he would be the most appropriate deputy and successor to Carol if there were to be one. Yet, when in the course of my interviews I asked the program directors about successors, not one of them ever mentioned Sam as a potential leader. I suspect that Sam had distorted the reality of his situation in his mind, not because he was grandiose, but because his close working relationship with Carol stimulated his fantasy that he was in fact special.

Now, remember that each person on the program staff had special access to Carol. If we assume that each of them, like Sam, imagined that he or she was Carol's favorite and a potential successor, it is not surprising that each would guard his or her link to Carol jealously. Their co-workers were potentially their competitors. Bill's position, even if it only hinted at the emergence of a deputy role, threatened to undermine each person's special access to the leader.

As a result of my interviews, I recommended that Carol institute a series of meetings with her six program directors. She would run the meetings, and Bill would be present. Up to that point, Carol had never held a meeting that distinguished one level of the agency from another—professionals, secretaries, and clerks all attended every meeting. I reasoned, and told her, that by holding a directors' meetings she would help the program directors differentiate themselves from the rest of the staff, and they would begin to feel more accountable for the work of their own subordinates and draw on one another rather than on her for advice. Such meetings, I thought, could create real relationships between Carol and her directors, replacing the fantasies of special relationships. Acknowledging that such meetings could fail, I suggested that Carol try holding them for three months and then meet with me and the program directors to assess them.

At the assessment meeting, Carol and the program directors reported that they had held three of the meetings I had recommended and had run into a problem. Carol noted that they had felt as if there were ghosts in the room: the absent members of the staff had seemed to haunt those present. They wondered if they could really hold any meeting of substance without including everybody.

An Episode of Competition

I facilitated a "debriefing" of the entire professional staff—that is, the program directors and the program managers who reported to them. This meeting, too, took place after the three-month experimental period, Marge, a program manager who officially reported to Sam, spoke up in anger. This whole process smacked of hierarchy, she noted; it went against the grain of the agency's egalitarian culture, and she had not been included in the decision to conduct the experiment. Moreover, she never considered herself to be Sam's subordinate, even if he formally appraised her performance once a year. She was his colleague.

Aware of Marge's anger before the meeting (for she had approached him to express her thoughts and feelings), Sam replied in a tense voice that he had in fact been supervising Marge's work, though he acknowledged he might have been lazy about this in the past because of Carol's close work with his staff. Carol replied a bit more testily, arguing that, no matter how Marge felt, Sam was her boss. I said that all three of them had contributed to this dilemma, and then I suggested that their long-standing three-level relationship probably typified some of the central dilemmas in the agency as a whole. Marge concurred, and then added that one reason she did not like these changes was that she found it very hard to give up her close relationship with Carol.

In effect, as Marge had stated, Sam was her colleague not her boss. But, as she also acknowledged, he was her competitor, potentially blocking her relationship with Carol. This suggests that Marge and the other members of the staff were willing to give up a lot of their own potential authority and forgo their own professional development— "become lazy," as Sam noted—if they could have a close and special relationship with Carol. Their willingness to forgo their own development, despite their competence and education, suggests that they not only idealized Carol but also identified with this idealization. They had come to believe that, simply by being and feeling close to Carol the leader, they could become the Carol they idealized. This is the way in which they managed their sense of dependence.

Feelings of Anger

A fantasy of anger played a critical role in shaping the way in which people at International Help felt about their interpersonal relationships. As we saw, Marge was angry at the potential loss of her position, though she had worked to control it by speaking with Sam before the "debriefing." However, I suggest that Carol and others had elaborated a fantasy in which angry and destructive feelings were always threatening to emerge throughout the agency.

As has already been noted, the program directors felt that in meeting with Carol and Bill they were confronting the ghosts of the absent staff members—as if by excluding them they had killed them, and these absent members were now returning like ghosts to wreak havoc. Equally striking was my own experience of appearing like a bad and terrible person who would wreak havoc on staff members. At the end of the debriefing I suggested that the program directors sponsor an all-staff meeting, to be held soon, in which the whole staff—non-professionals included—could assess the work that had taken place during the consultation. Carol hastily replied that this would not be possible, arguing that some of the people would not want me there.

I had a quick flash of a scene, which I imagined was in Carol's mind, in which my presence would stimulate program staffers to attack me—that is, I imagined that in Carol's mind I was a potentially hated person. I remember feeling angry and blurting out to Carol "Aren't these your meetings?" She responded somewhat huffily that indeed they were. Catching myself, I said that I didn't want to argue with her but I would like to think out loud for a moment. I said that to come to "take on the staff, like a showdown at the OK Corral" would be foolish of me, and grandiose to boot. I then told Carol that through much of the consultation she had seemed to want to keep me away from the staff. I said I felt that she was excluding me from a staff process as if I were dangerous or poisonous. She said that she *did* feel that way, and I then said that perhaps the staffers needed to talk with me directly so that the difficulties I seemed to represent could be faced more directly. After all, I added, I was not so bad in the flesh. A new program director then chuckled, noting that she had heard all about this strange person from the local business school (where I was teaching at the time), but that meeting me hadn't been so bad. Carol then agreed to invite me to the meeting and to talk ahead of time to any staffers who might have trouble with my presence.

As it turned out, my presence at the all-staff meeting stimulated serious and sometimes difficult talk, but certainly no explosive attacks on me or anyone else. I suggest that Carol's fantasy of the ghosts' returning and her image of either my destructiveness or my vulnerability to attack highlighted an underlying tone and mood at the agency. People walked carefully around one another, fearful of stimulating the anxiety and anger they all felt in competing for access to the prized leader. To support Carol as the sole authority, they had to distance themselves from one another and consequently construct a somewhat isolating and hostile group life. In denying their own dependence, they created a fragile and tentative group culture.

I witnessed a poignant consequence of this isolation when, in the final meeting of the consultation, I again met with Carol, Bill, and the program directors. Bill sought feedback and discussion of his role. He asked the group what his role in the program directors' meeting might be in the future. If the meeting were to take on decision-making responsibilities, would he have a say, or (since he did not directly supervise professionals but was rather Carol's assistant) would his primary role to be to support the meeting?

No one answered Bill, and he seemed alone and unsupported at that moment. It was clear that, by isolating Bill, the program directors could feel less vulnerable. They could protect their special relationships with Carol by transferring their sense of vulnerability onto

Bill, by keeping him uncertain. I told the group that Bill's problem of clarifying his role was not unlike the problem the whole agency had in differentiating roles and drawing boundaries. Still no one answered Bill. I turned to Bill and noted that his question reflected the continuing difficulty he faced in defining his role. I then turned to the group as a whole and noted that it was very hard to say "no" aloud in this organization. But all this was to no avail. One program director turned to Bill and said: "We will have to see how this meeting evolves. This is an evolutionary process." I then said that the group was avoiding the issue, and they had all learned to become good diplomats. Bill smiled and said: "Yes, we are all diplomats." The meeting ended shortly afterward.

In short, Bill could not get an honest and direct discussion of his role. The program directors wanted to isolate him, but I suspect that their avoiding him also reflected the wariness they felt for one another. Fearful of stimulating overt competition, they were unable to treat one another seriously and honestly. Consequently, group life had a somewhat ascetic and emotionally denuded quality. Although the feel of the group was serious, committed, and intellectual, it lacked the elemental qualities of fun and nurturing that help groups through difficult times.

Paradoxically, because the employees of International Help attempted to dispense with hierarchy, they intensified their dependence on their leader, competed with their peers to get access to her, and hobbled the peers they scapegoated. As the weakened formal role system failed to channel feelings of dependence, a pervasive and at times insidious psychological process took hold in which individuals could convert the reality of their increasing dependence into a fantasy of their specialness. They regressed emotionally, and the organization could not draw on the full measure of their talents.

The Paradox of Personalization

By depersonalizing relationships, by putting individuals in roles within a hierarchy, the modern organization helped people channel certain feelings (such as the wish to do good work) while suppressing other feelings (such as resenting one's own low status). One could maintain some emotional distance from the role one occupied. Today individuals need to personalize their work relationships, and this means relaxing the hierarchy and giving them greater freedom to negotiate their roles and to express their talents.

But, as the case of International Help suggests, once we personalize relationships and unleash the genie of affect we take the risk of provoking feelings that people cannot contain. If once employees could manage their feelings of dependence by experiencing their dependent relationships in social or class terms, now they must experience these feelings as reflections of their character, their personhood. This sets the stage for emotional regression. Unable to contain these feelings, people seek solace or flight in fantasies that contradict their experience. In the case of International Help, people could transform their experience of dependence into one of uniqueness. The freedom that personalization has offered has been debased; gold has turned into lead.

To prevent regression and promote personal and organizational development, we need a deeper understanding of the psychodynamics of personalization. How can and should the leader personalize his or her role in ways that help followers successfully personalize their roles? How does a post-modern hierarchy help us become persons to one another while allowing us to contain feelings that might undermine the work we have to accomplish?

3

Envy

I have suggested that in the post-modern organization leaders must make themselves more psychologically present. This means that leaders can no longer suppress their passions and beliefs; instead they must find ways of expressing them so that other individuals can fully understand what matters to them and why. In settings of high uncertainty, subordinates must know what risks their leader wishes to take and why. This information will not necessarily clarify the structures or the potential impacts of new technologies or new competitors, but it does clarify where and how much the leader will extend himself or herself to develop strategies or find solutions.

In revealing their passions, however, leaders make themselves vulnerable. They demonstrate what they care about and how their failure or their organization's failure would hurt them. But they also make themselves more transparent and accessible—and this in turn helps followers trust them more. Many leaders cannot reveal themselves in this way, however. Without conscious awareness that they are doing so, some mask themselves with bravado; some appear terrifying; some become "cheerleaders"; some appear fragile and easily hurt. In each case, the leader's persona, rather than his person, defines and limits the working relationships he can develop with others. This impedes everyone's work.

The leader's passion about work plays a crucial role in containing normal disruptions of group life, particularly the competitiveness and envy that accompany the work of every team. Consultants often like to paint a world in which perfect team members, without an ounce of self-centeredness, feel no rivalry with anyone. As we have seen, this is a fantasy. An organization is effective only because individuals have various talents, some more highly developed than others. The array of talents is the rational basis for the division of labor and the ground for the inevitable differences in status and prestige that accompany organizational life. I have already assessed the impact of these differences on how people manage their feelings of dependency. Here I want to focus on how these differences stimulate envy and its vicissitudes.

Differences in talent, competence, or achievements can make people feel weak, insufficient, and vulnerable. Let me give a personal example: I sought help on a difficult consultation from my colleague Nancy. My client, the head of a consulting company, wanted me to conduct a retreat with him and his partners, yet after I interviewed the individuals I came to believe that a retreat would not be useful. The partners appeared to be isolated from one another and emotionally detached from my client. The interviews I conducted were not easy; some of the partners clearly were withholding information and feelings from me. Nancy asked me several pointed questions and quickly developed a diagnosis that helped me articulate my own feelings. Curiously, her help also stung. Although I felt helped, I also felt a bit diminished. Why? In seeking help I felt vulnerable. Nancy's effectiveness then confirmed my weakness, and I could not help but compare myself to her. Why was she so "smart" and why was I so "stupid?" When people feel stung or belittled, some become envious. Feeling envious, they can then develop contempt for the gifts and talents of others, pretending that these are signs of some secret flaws in the gifted person. This stimulates rivalry, makes the envious ones feel less vulnerable, and often leads them to undermine the very people on whom they depend.[1]

The leader plays a critical role here. By projecting passion and making himself vulnerable, a leader helps his followers focus less on their rivalries and more on him as a representative of the group's main task. Differences in talent can be tolerated because everyone has a felt stake in the group's and the leader's effectiveness and success. The followers will feel less diminished by their differences if the leader makes himself more open to the followers. This works, however, only to the degree that the leader tolerates his own vulnerability and allows it to emerge. Ironically, in situations of ambiguous

1. This concept of envy has been developed at great length by Melanie Klein. See, for example, *Envy and Gratitude and Other Works, 1946–1963* (Dell, 1975).

authority (for example, where multilevel meetings are common and a unit leader's subordinates may work with the leader's boss), people in leadership positions may feel increasingly vulnerable. They are living in a fishbowl. Since the post-modern organization thrives on the ability of individuals to negotiate their roles and their authority depending on the task, it seems as if the post-modern organization creates a contradiction: Can a leader project openness while feeling more exposed than ever? If not, might not the leader suppress his passion, thereby letting loose feelings of envy and rivalry that will ultimately undermine the organization's performance? Consider the following example.

Example: Good Care Hospital

Barry, the chief operating officer of Good Care Hospital, and Dave, the chief executive officer, had a close working relationship. Both were in their mid forties and were well respected by other hospital administrators and by attending physicians. The hospital—the flagship of the four-hospital Good Care Health System—was the premier tertiary-care institution in its region. Most of its beds were occupied and returned considerable revenue to the Good Care Health System.

Dave, though still officially CEO of Good Care Hospital, spent most of his time in his new role as a vice-president in the Good Care Health System. He worked in the system office on a wide range of strategic issues, such as the contracting of managed care and the integration of operating systems across the four hospitals. Thus, he could not attend to the day-to-day operation of Good Care Hospital with any regularity. Hence, Barry, the COO, had considerable discretion and authorization to reshape the hospital's services so that cost increases were limited while quality was maintained. Shortly after joining the hospital, Barry had reorganized its operations to highlight three "magnet" programs: cardiac care, women's and children's services, and emergency services. These services, he believed, would generate the bulk of the hospital's revenue while sustaining its ability to compete.

Barry's top team included the managers of the three magnet programs, the manager of the general medical surgical floors, and others who were in charge of staff functions such as facilities management, marketing, and finance. The team also included one person in charge of developing a cancer program and another who headed the hospital's ancillary services. Some of these managers had once reported to Dave, but they now all reported to Barry. Only the chief financial officer and the physician liaison reported to Dave. Barry was, increasingly, functioning as the de facto CEO of the hospital.

The Top Team and Its Dynamics

Despite ample evidence of their success, the members of the top team complained chronically, both in public and in private, that as a team they did not feel effective. Each understood his or her own function and role, but their collaboration seemed wanting. They appeared confused about the links between magnet programs and support and ancillary services. How were the latter supposed to support the magnet programs? In addition, while the team members appeared to respect Barry, they felt that the team lacked soul and passion. They pointed to their semimonthly meeting, which Dave officially chaired but Barry ran, as evidence that they were not functioning effectively. The meeting too often felt flat, and team members worried that hidden agendas or unexpressed personal hostility were quashing their spirits.

In our consultation to Good Care Hospital, we had occasion to work with the top team and thereby stumble into their troublesome psychodynamics. At the retreat reported on here, we found that the dynamics of envy were inhibiting the team's functioning. Most important, we came to believe that Barry was uncertain about how to exercise his authority in front of Dave. Barry's resulting feelings of vulnerability led him to attenuate his psychological presence when working with team members. Lacking a sense of what Barry cared about, of what motivated him, his subordinates became more rivalrous with one another. In short, the group was fractured and subject to the pressure of envy and jealousy precisely because Barry, feeling exposed in the semi-monthly meeting, could not invest his role with his qualities as a person.

A Retreat

In order to understand the dynamics of this process, let us examine a retreat that Barry sponsored to review the hospital's strategy and to help members of the top team better understand their functioning as a group. Barry believed that some team members had not internalized the hospital's strategy, and he was certainly aware of the discontent among the members. He hoped that, in clarifying the hospital's strategy, team members would better understand their individual and collective roles.

One way of grasping the dynamics of a team is to look broadly at the context, at the structure of reporting relationships, at the team's key tasks, and at the strengths, weaknesses, and proclivities of the members. Another is to examine a slice of the team's actual process of working. In psychodynamic consulting, we assume that when people come together to work on important issues they reproduce in their conversations the most important dynamics of their relationships. This "process view" changes our mode of analysis. Instead of looking at the broad picture, we pay close attention to the details of what people say, when, and to whom. We assume that the way a conversation unfolds provides important clues to what is uppermost in the participants' minds. We also pay attention to who has not spoken and to what topics are missing from the conversation. In line with what has been noted in this paragraph, the focus of my discussion of Good Care Hospital will shift from broad themes to details that reveal these themes.

The first day
The retreat was to take place over an afternoon, an evening, and the next day. Dave was to join the team members for dinner and remain with them for the second day.

Barry planned to spend the first afternoon reviewing the significance of the hospital's magnet services. He also planned to discuss why some of the hospital's services might need more capital for expansion while others might have to reduce costs. He believed that if managers understood which of these two tasks they were likely to face they would understand how to take up their roles.

To prepare for the retreat, Barry had created a complex chart in which departments were listed across the columns and key strategic parameters—market size, capital requirements, revenue and expenses, competitive pressures—were listed down the rows. Each person on the team was asked to assess how his or her particular function or department should affect or be affected by these parameters and why. Should the department grow, should it reduce costs, should it obtain more or less new capital over time?

I was initially excited by Barry's chart; it gave the team members a framework for assessing the hospital's strategy and challenged them to specify their roles in helping the hospital achieve its goals. I felt that it offered a vehicle for linking strategy questions (such as "Where is this hospital going?") to role questions ("What role do I play on this team to help the hospital succeed?"). In addition, the chart helped people avoid the trap of speaking in generalities by making them focus directly on efforts to expand capacity or control costs.

Surprisingly, the afternoon's conversation was dull and dry. People appeared listless, they talked to satisfy Barry, and Barry seemed burdened. When Barry challenged an assumption that Jane, the head of the medical and surgical units in the hospital, had made, Jane responded: "Whatever you say, Barry." Toward the end of the afternoon, Mary (who was in charge of developing a cancer center) and Barry engaged in an endless debate. There was passion in it, but it felt like a ritual. After the meeting Mary told me that she felt that the team had isolated and abandoned her. She worried that in arguing with Barry she was exposing herself to unnecessary risk. I said that it seemed as if the team had nominated her to keep Barry busy with arguments as the rest of them withdrew. "Sometimes," I said to Mary, "you have to throw a dog a bone."

The consultants too felt frustrated, and at the end of the afternoon's session we decided to interpret the feel of the day's work to the top team. We suggested that the meeting's dullness signified that the group had attacked Barry's authority. After all, we noted, they had disregarded his chart and the important thinking it represented. Predictably, this interpretation had little impact. The group appeared as uninterested in our thoughts as they were in Barry's. Indeed, one member told me later that upon hearing our interpretation she had thought to herself "Where are these guys coming from?"

People then retired to dinner in a dimly lit room with two tables. Some of the managers gathered around Barry at one table. Dave came in and sat with other managers at the second table. I and my co-consultant sat with Dave. As we talked with him, the conversation at the other table grew animated and intense. It seemed as if the

Table 3.1
The members of the Good Care management team and their roles.

Barry	Chief operating officer
Dave	Chief executive officer
Henry	Chief financial officer
Laura	Manager, Cardiac Care Services
Joe	Manager, Women's and Children's Services
Jill	Manager, Marketing
Mary	Manager, Cancer Care Program
Fred	Manager, Emergency Services
Robert	Medical Liaison
Marla	Manager, Ancillary Services
Jane	Managing Nurse, General Medical and Surgical Units
Sam	Director of Human Resources

work they had been unable to accomplish in the afternoon might now be taking place.

We described the afternoon to Dave, and he said he was aware that it had not gone well. Speaking elusively, he noted that he had heard some concerns about the top team. "People have spoken," he said, as if something dishonest or unscrupulous was taking place in the group. He really wanted to get this aired. We pushed the two dinner tables together, and I asked the people at Barry's table to report on what they had been discussing at dinner.

Below is a synopsis of the ensuing conversation. It is not a verbatim record; rather, it summarizes the key points and the sequence in which they were made. (Table 3.1 identifies the roles of the team members.)

Dave: Let's get our difficulties aired.

Consultant: Let's put the two tables together. What were you were talking about at your table, Barry?

Barry: People said that I should stop always defending Laura.

Jane: Laura, how did you feel about people's attitudes toward you?

Laura: At meetings I am always getting these "nonverbals" [i.e., "dirty looks"].

Consultant: The group is trying to understand Laura's experience. . . .

Joe: I think in general that people on the team do not pay enough attention to each other.

Jill (with anger): My people are very frustrated working with Laura's staff. They are not involved early enough. They don't have this problem with other departments.

Laura (to Jill): We have different marketing needs now then we used to have. We don't need help with concepts anymore, just help in execution.

Barry: The magnet program managers have different styles, particularly in the way they use staff resources.

Mary: Laura, Joe—what is it like to be held so responsible for the hospital's bottom line?

Laura: When I look at the size of my numbers, I get nervous.

Joe: It can feel very lonely.

Barry: I picked the magnet group leaders because they can act independently. [He then describes in some detail the process by which he picked them.]

Barry (with passion): I am focusing on Cardiac Services because the leadership at the last hospital I worked was not responsible. They had to lay off 175 people. *I can't let this happen here.*

Consultant: Barry, people rarely hear you talk so passionately.

Jill: Yes, it was good to hear you speak this way, Barry. Most of the time we just hear you talk numbers.

This synopsis reveals an interesting pattern:

• Barry answers my opening question by noting in a *mea culpa* fashion that he had been told by the group that he must stop continually defending Laura (the manager of Cardiac Care, the most profitable service). The group, he noted at dinner, felt that he favored her too much. By highlighting this part of the dinner conversation, Barry communicates that this was indeed its most important part. The issue of Laura, he says, lies at the heart of the group's discontent.

• Jane then turns to Laura and asks her how she feels. (Whether she means now or in general is ambiguous.) Laura highlights the sense that she is held in suspicion by noting that at many staff meetings she gets lots of "nonverbals" from people, as if she were doing something wrong. I then note that the group appears to be trying to understand Laura's experience. Perhaps, I add (probably not too helpfully at this point), the group has produced a vicious circle of behavior: Laura is excluded, and then it appears that she has set herself apart as if she is special and favored.

• Joe notes that people on the team are not paying attention to one another. He is suggesting that Laura may not be the only one who feels isolated or different. Since Joe heads the Women's and Children's magnet program, he is most likely communicating that he too faces problems with the group. In other words, the problem lies not with Laura but with the role of manager of a magnet program.

• Jill, who appears angry at Laura, resists the implications of Joe's statement. She wants to keep the conversation focused on Laura. She notes that Laura's people, in contrast to others in line units, do not work with her own staff collaboratively. Laura's people, Jill says, just tell her staff what do. In effect, Jill notes that she feels diminished by Laura. Laura responds that she now has different needs for help from marketing. Because Cardiac Care Services now understands its market, it needs less conceptual assistance and more help in executing certain marketing tasks.

• Barry, having already noted that he is not supposed to defend Laura, now defends her. He notes that each magnet program director has a different management style, particularly in regard to the use of staff resources. He accepts these differences, he says, and the remaining members of the team must learn to adapt to them. Thus, the members of the group enact this basic pattern: They try to punish Laura by rejecting her, and Barry asserts her significance by discounting their critique. Of course, this makes team members feel that "Barry is always defending Laura"—proof that she has unearned status on the team.

• Barry's defense shifts the group's attention from Laura. Some team members may have simply decided "it is not worth fighting this one"; however, Mary (as her next comments indicate) uses Barry's comment as a springboard for further understanding the roles of the magnet program managers. She asks both Laura and Joe how it feels to be so responsible for the hospital's bottom line. This is a turning point in the conversation. By asking Joe as well as Laura, Mary affirms Barry's shift away from Laura while suggesting (as Joe did earlier) that Laura's predicament reflects something about her role as the director of a key hospital program. Laura and Joe then both report that they feel burdened by their responsibilities. Mary, who earlier had engaged in a ritual fight with Barry, now collaborates with him to deepen the conversation. Her strong link to Barry—perhaps her identification with him—explains why she might be the team's main "fighter" against him as well as his primary collaborator.

• Barry, feeling supported by Mary, now feels free to explain why he chose the various magnet group managers. He emphasizes that he selected them for their independence—for their ability to shoulder responsibility and risk alone. In others words, Barry suggests that he wants Laura, Joe, and Fred to be able to stand on their own, *to be isolated in some degree.* Note here that Barry takes the risk of provoking competitive feelings (as he no doubt did) because Mary's support has freed him to talk more directly and with less hesitance.

• Then, in an important moment, Barry's tone of voice shifts from the matter-of-fact to the passionate. He notes that he had chosen to focus on Cardiac Care Services in particular because "the leadership at the last hospital I worked at, was not responsible" and "they had to lay off 175 people." In other words, Barry brought his feelings and experience to his rationale for focusing on Cardiac Care Services. He would not let the hospital lose essential resources; he was going to protect his own employees. That is why he needed Laura's management and business skills.

• I then said to Barry that people rarely heard him speak so passionately. Jill concurred, saying she felt good hearing Barry speak in this way when most of the time "we just hear [him] talk numbers." In other words, Jill was suggesting that she now understood the difference between the afternoon and post-dinner conversations. In the afternoon, people could feel free to reject Barry's authority because he did not link his strategic choices to his passion. He was all "numbers." After dinner, for the first time, he appeared less aloof; his analytic skills were linked to his capacity to care. Jill's statement is particularly striking since it was she who appeared most angry at Laura and presumably at Barry. Barry's passion allows her to reorganize her feelings about his leadership. In turn, this could help her resent Laura less.

The vignette thus far highlights the interplay between role and person. The group believes that Laura is an uppity person and is responsible for her own isolation. They believe that, for personal reasons, Barry favors her unfairly. The conversation helps the group create a different hypothesis, that the role of a magnet program manager is distinctive and that, to some degree, it psychologically isolates those who occupy it. The group had overpersonalized Laura's behavior, and as a consequence scapegoated her. The members need to depersonalize their experience of her.

Barry's passion highlights a different dynamic of role and person. By talking "numbers," Barry had depersonalized his role, making it difficult for people to understand the rationale for his choices. Thus, Barry's self-willed depersonalization and Laura's overpersonalized status are linked In addition, because team members have stereotyped Laura, she feels depersonalized and inhibited. Lacking in each case is the appropriate role-person balance. The case of Good Care, as I have described it thus far, points to at least two ways in which the imbalance is expressed: denying the significance of a role in one's behavior and denying one's person in taking up a role.

The case thus far also helps us understand the psychodynamics of envy in a team. Overpersonalizing Laura's behavior makes it easy to resent her status. But, as I have just argued, one reason Laura was rejected was that Barry lacked passion. This suggests that rivalry and envy can be contained when the leader brings more of his person to his role. Because Barry had not projected his personal authority into his plan and his strategy for the hospital, there seemed to be something abstract about his commitment. This abstract quality enabled people to resist his authority, which is why they were compliant in the afternoon's discussion. By discounting Barry, team members could give expression to their feelings of envy and rivalry. In order to sublimate their competitive feelings, they needed Barry's passion. This idea also helps to explain the role Mary played earlier in the day: the group nominated her to produce some superficial "heat" to compensate for Barry's psychological withdrawal.

The second day

The second day's effort, an all-day meeting, extended the work of the previous day while providing the team with greater insight into the dilemmas Barry faced in bringing his person to his role.

Fred, the head of Emergency Services, was given an opportunity to discuss his experience in his role. Like Joe and Laura, he noted that he had felt alone. At that point, the magnet program managers had been re-integrated into the group and each had been given a chance to talk about his or her sense of isolation and burden. The realization that they shared similar experiences underlined the importance of their role.

Some time after Fred spoke, Robert (the one physician on the team) asked Barry to discuss how he saw his own role. This question triggered a very important conversation. Team members began discussing how they experienced Barry, particularly at the semi-monthly all-staff meetings. As has already been mentioned, Dave officially chaired that meeting but Barry was responsible for the agenda. Barry, they felt, controlled the meeting too tightly. His frequent demand for "completed staff work" led people to feel that they could present only the most ironclad of arguments. They felt that all questions had to be resolved with arguments and recommendations before the meeting. This suppressed spontaneity and turned presentations into performances.

Barry responded by explaining what he meant by "completed staff work." He felt that without rigor and precision the meeting would be unproductive. Marla, the head of ancillary services, responded that at the weekly breakfast meeting, convened by Barry for the purpose of discussing operational issues, the participants (including a subset of the team members who attended the semi-monthly meeting) spoke with spontaneity and humor. Whereas the semi-monthly meeting often felt lifeless, the operations meeting felt spontaneous and vital.

This discussion led Marla to an important insight. She suggested that perhaps Barry controlled the semi-monthly meeting so tightly because he did not want to be embarrassed in front of Dave. If Barry's subordinates' work was not complete, she said, Dave might think that Barry himself was careless. Neither Barry nor Dave responded, but they appeared to be listening carefully. Then Jane noted that Marla's comment made a lot of sense. I pointed out that multi-level meetings where subordinates and superiors are in the same room often prove difficult. The group members then relaxed, and the meeting ended with members laughing at past events and anticipating future ones.

Marla's comment deepened the team's understanding of Barry's behavior. Barry had a penchant for technical thinking, and his communication through numbers was undoubtedly part of the way in which he took up his role. But his complex relationship with Dave reinforced his tendency to withdraw behind numbers and behind the precision of completed staff work. The group's process thus revealed the sequence of relationships illustrated in figure 3.1. Barry inhibited the projection of his own passion. Feeling vulnerable in front of Dave, Barry retreated to abstractions (numbers), and team members, unable to identify with these numbers alone, let loose their competitive feelings. Consequently, the team members envied Laura, Fred, and Joe (Joe was central to implementing Barry's strategy) while failing to acknowledge the particular burdens and risks the magnet program managers faced. But by withholding their emotional support for these managers and their programs, the team members could not, as a consequence, identify emotionally with

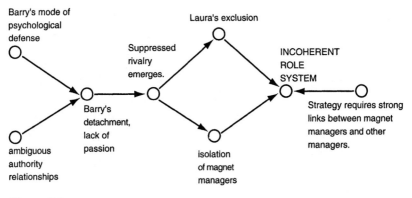

Figure 3.1

Barry's strategy for the hospital. This is why they felt detached from their own roles and estranged from the team.

This case highlights the distinctive role that leaders' passions play in work groups. Each member of a work group brings a wide variety of feelings, experiences, and values to the work. Some are disappointed in their careers; many bring the feelings of rivalry they first experienced in their families; others feel chronically diminished by those who are more talented. This is the irreducible human element of organizational life. However, the members of a well-functioning group suppress certain elements of this background of experience in the interests of supporting the group's work and the leader's purposes. In other words, people can feel intense about their work—can bring their passion to their work—if the leader's passion helps them overcome the sense that they have been diminished and made vulnerable by the talents of others.

Conclusion

Let us return to the theme of our book. We want leaders to be open, but, facing this prospect and its attendant difficulties, leaders may instead detach themselves emotionally from their work and their roles. Like Barry in the example above, many leaders face a challenge of managing their sense of vulnerability. Hoping to stimulate participation, openness, and broad thinking, senior executives are increasingly sponsoring multi-level meetings and retreats. Moreover, as organizations work to integrate their many disparate functions and levels, it is not uncommon for executives (like Dave in the example) to occupy more than one executive role, or for managers to be the leaders of "cross-functional" groups that include their superiors. We are losing the comfort that the simple hierarchy once provided. Executives feel increasingly vulnerable to scrutiny, evaluation, and assessment by their subordinates as well as their superiors. Threatened by these conditions, executives may retreat behind their roles, thereby depriving the organization of the energy, commitment, and passion it most requires.

4

Abdication

The case of Good Care Hospital highlights the ambiguous heritage that hierarchy has left us. In the modern organization, individuals could use hierarchy to suppress the parts of themselves that interfered with their work. Today we know that we must personalize our roles if we are to work successfully. As we build non-hierarchical arrangements, such as cross-level task forces and cross-functional work teams, leaders and followers feel less protected. If they are not prepared, they will respond not with more openness but (as we saw in chapter 3 in the case of the Good Care team) with withdrawal and regression. What is the appropriate role of hierarchy in a post-modern organization? What is a post-modern hierarchy?

In exploring this question, we should pay particular attention to the abdication of leaders. Barry, the COO of Good Care Hospital, withdrew emotionally but remained committed to his task. He attenuated his passion but did not abandon his work. When leaders abdicate, they abandon the work itself. They no longer face the challenge of balancing role and person, because they have psychologically relinquished their roles. In doing so, they retreat from hierarchy while embracing bureaucracy. They abdicate by substituting rules and procedures for judgment and relationships.

Hierarchy

The chain of command is a time-tested tool for delegating authority while not abdicating leadership. Today, the word "hierarchy" conjures up images of control and suppression. A hierarchy has another aspect, however. Although it creates a system in which some roles are vested with more authority than others (this is the "anti-democratic" aspect), it also facilitates delegation. It allows leaders to "lend" their authority to subordinates, thereby enabling the subordinates to participate in the leadership process.

In a rational system of delegation the leader is supported by followers who take up leadership roles protecting parts of the organization so that the leader can attend to the whole. The leader willingly becomes dependent on followers and vulnerable to their mistakes because he or she is confident in the capacity of the entire organization to spot errors before they turn into disasters.

But a leaders who is frightened by the external risks his organization faces, or who feels poorly equipped do to the job, may overcontrol his followers as a substitute for controlling external reality. In such a situation, the leader may violate the chain of command by failing to delegate. Alternatively, the leader may unconsciously build in his mind a fantasized "participative culture" so as to share the enterprise's risks with the followers without acknowledging his genuine dependence on them. Thus, by abdicating, either an apparently overcontrolling or an apparently democratic one may be managing his own vulnerability.

Bureaucracy

Bureaucracy, unlike hierarchy, is a particularly powerful mechanism for fostering abdication while masking it. The bureaucracy depersonalizes decision making so that individuals at different levels of authority can simply follow rules. They lose the sense of personal accountability for the decisions they make, and therefore they feel less responsible for the unpredictable consequences of these decisions. A leader who does this gains anonymity, which is the first step toward abdication, but then can no longer use the chain of command to share his leadership. Authority is now vested in rules rather than relationships, and a leader hoping to manage his own vulnerability actually makes the organization more vulnerable. The following example shows how the bureaucratic escape route promotes abdication.

Example: Ocean Reactor

Ocean Reactor, a nuclear power plant built in the 1970s and owned by a small utility company, supplied a significant amount of electricity to the company's customers and contributed significantly to its profits. The plant's managers faced increasing difficulties in managing it efficiently. The number of unplanned outages grew, the workers took more and more time to shut down and start up the reactor, and maintenance work increased. My colleagues and I were asked to assess the organizational issues and to suggest changes in structure, roles, or responsibilities that might improve the plant's performance.

Interviews suggested that all power plant managers and workers faced the problem of using an increasingly complex set of procedures to guide their work. Before the 1979 accident at Three Mile Island, workers in most nuclear power plants could exercise considerable discretion in accomplishing their tasks. They had to strictly follow emergency operating procedures, but there were only broad guidelines for other work (such as bringing a pump on line, testing equipment, or replacing a valve). Before Three Mile Island, procedures for such activities were written out as "step lists," and an operator did not have to follow them in sequence. But after Three Mile Island the U.S. Nuclear Regulatory Commission encouraged utility managers to develop procedures for a wide range of tasks that were to be implemented only in one way and through one sequence. In the decade after Three Mile Island, Ocean Reactor's managers developed more than 500 operating procedures, 600 test performance procedures, and hundreds of maintenance procedures.

The Limits of Procedures

The new system of procedures for operating and maintaining Ocean Reactor proved increasingly burdensome. Top management evolved a philosophy they called "verbatim compliance." Workers and supervisors had to comply with the "letter of the law" and implement procedures without deviating from them in any detail. This philosophy, combined with the procedures, posed great difficulties. Because thousands of work steps were covered, any set of articulated procedures was inevitably incomplete, contradictory, and inaccurate. During a particular incident at Ocean Reactor, for instance, maintenance workers needed to lift some wires to repair a motor but discovered that the written procedures did not specify how to perform this step. To complete their work, the mechanics lifted the wire. Subsequently, the technicians assigned to test the motor before it was put back on line found that the testing procedures did not cover the situation in which maintenance workers had lifted the wires. Since a procedure writer cannot anticipate all situations and conditions that shape an operator's or a mechanic's work, errors of omission arise. Thus, the procedures are often incomplete, and this forces the operator to act outside the mandate of "verbatim compliance."

Fear and Uncertainty

These lapses in consistency, completeness, and accuracy made it hard for operators, mechanics, and their supervisors to understand management's philosophy of verbatim compliance. If a procedure is wrong or incomplete, or if it contradicts another, what should mechanics or operators do? Would they be chastised or disciplined if they followed a bad procedure or corrected it? One high-level manager noted: "Responsibility for success or failure in implementing a procedure is on the operator right now. If he violates a procedure, even if he's right, he's wrong. If he doesn't violate a procedure and it's wrong, he's wrong."

Such dilemmas naturally burdened operators, mechanics, and technicians, who were well aware of the moral and profession burdens they bore in acting responsibly despite the uncertainty they faced. Moreover, as licensed professionals, they could be personally fined for errors they made. A health physics technician, responsible for ensuring the safety of mechanics working near or around sources of radiation, noted that he could be fined when a supervisor's error led to excessive exposure of an employee. The organization as a whole neither supported nor protected the operators or the technicians. By relying on procedures and on a philosophy of verbatim compliance, top management reduced the workers' discretion in their roles while creating a climate in which they felt—and in fact were—personally vulnerable and exposed.

The system was not entirely inflexible. Operators, mechanics, and technicians could request a temporary procedure revision (TPR) to correct a procedure they deemed inappropriate. But this process proved cumbersome, making it difficult for workers to complete their assignments on time. Under the pressure of deadlines, supervisors often discouraged operators from requesting a TPR or encouraged them to note on the TPR that they were not asking for any change to the "intent" of a procedure. The latter reduced the time supervisors spent reviewing the document and the time management spent later in addressing the procedure's overall validity. Of course, as operators and managers defined a growing number of procedural deviations as consistent with original intent, the gap between the actual work system and the official procedural system grew.

The Balancing Act

Confronting incomplete, inaccurate procedures or procedures that contradicted others, workers and supervisors developed a covert work system that established an effective balance among the philosophy of verbatim compliance, the normal pressures of production, and the unpredictable contingencies of operating and maintaining a nuclear reactor. They "did what the boss wants, not what he said." They subverted formal management processes to meet management's expectations, thereby creating an enduring set of tensions. Alluding to these tensions, one manager suggested that "the next major accident in the nuclear industry [after Three Mile Island] will be caused by operators' following procedures." The very system created to contain and control risk was creating new dangers.

The Organizational Structure

One might imagine that these dilemmas are simply outgrowths of the technology's complexity and danger. This is hardly the case. Both the organization's structure and its process reinforced these dilemmas and blocked their resolution.

The organization was divided into three parts: an Operations group (responsible for producing power), a Maintenance group, and a Central Services group (responsible for writing procedures and enforcing health physics regulations). The chief operating officer, Jack, who reported to the corporate office, ostensibly oversaw and integrated the work of these three divisions. Yet he was so preoccupied with broader business and regulatory issues that he failed to keep track of daily operations. Instead, people look to Brad,[1] the head of Operations, as the power plant's unofficial manager, since he was responsible for power production. But unlike a true general manager, Brad did not formally supervise the other two managers (i.e., those of Maintenance and Central Services) and was not authorized to resolve conflicts among the three divisions. In consequence, though he was regarded as the unofficial head of the plant, Brad did not have formal authority to resolve differences among the divisions.

Checks and Balances

Instead, managers indicated that their organizational process was based on the principle of *checks and balances*. This is a suggestive term. Used to characterize the U.S. federal government, it describes a system in which no branch or division has power over the others. Instead, each constrains or checks the other, ensuring that power and authority are never concentrated in one branch. Checks and balances is thus a quintessential *political* principle implemented to prevent tyranny. In this sense it is inherently an anti-hierarchical principle. When implemented in an enterprise, it prevents any one manager from representing the interests and goals of the organization as a whole.

While preventing tyranny, checks and balances provoked a great deal of mistrust and suspicion between Ocean Reactor's divisions, and defensive behavior on the part of each. Since the division managers felt authorized to check one another, each assumed that the employees in the other divisions were in fact irresponsible and had to be checked. During our initial interviews, people throughout the plant described their function as checking the other groups. For example, Operations employees believed that they had to prevent Maintenance from tying up the reactor; safety workers believed that they had prevent Maintenance supervisors from overexposing workers to radiation; and Operations people believed that they had to prevent safety workers from delaying maintenance. Rather than support one another, each division's manager prevented the others from doing damage.

1. Brad was my client.

A health physics supervisor described a typical pattern. The health physics workers felt that their role was to check the "irresponsible" behavior of Maintenance supervisors. They were therefore conservative in estimating the length of time a worker could spend in an area exposed to radiation. The Maintenance supervisors, who felt pressed by Operations supervisors to complete their work, resented this constraint on their capacity to deploy workers. They, in turn, subverted the goals of the health physics group by simply putting more workers on the job than was customary, thus limiting each worker's exposure but increasing the total number of workers exposed to health hazards. When the health physics supervisor discovered this, his belief that Maintenance supervisors had to be carefully monitored was reinforced.

Similarly, one supervisor from Central Services described how a "test and performance" technician determined that a recently repaired component could not be put back into operation because it had failed a performance test. However, the senior watch supervisor, though required to complete a report on the test failure, refused to do so because it would delay refueling. Since the component had only barely failed, he ordered another test for the next morning. Such incidents only reinforced the test and performance technicians' beliefs that they had to be tough on Operations to protect the integrity of the equipment.

Because the system of checks and balances increased inter-divisional conflict, people throughout the organization felt that they were working in an overly politicized system. This is reflected in the following comments: "We work here along divisional lines; we need a team concept." "There is no structure here for conflict resolution." "We alienate the team concept here; a good baseball team does not have checks and balances."

These statements are provocative. They suggest that people in the plant consider a well-functioning hierarchy to be a precondition for teamwork. In a hierarchy, the general manager contains the potential conflicts between divisions by representing the interests and goals of the entire organization. This leadership work of containing and integrating then enables people from different divisions to work together without stumbling into conflicts over basic priorities. The hierarchy enables top management to represent the whole organization to its members. Buttressed with such a conception of the whole, people are free to exercise their initiative in working across divisions and groups. No longer consumed by the politics of their organization, they can focus on the task.

One manager at Ocean Reactor described the origins and implications of the checks-and-balances system beautifully:

> Our work in the fossil stations was totally different. The plant manager made clear that there was a prime directive [in force]. Everything was treated on a plant-wide basis. Basically, your role was to make the plant manager look good. If I was a supervisor and didn't identify a components problem by Friday afternoon, then I got yelled at for spending overtime dollars. Here at Ocean Reactor we yell at Maintenance people for working overtime.

This statement highlights three interrelated issues. First, in a well-functioning hierarchy there is a chain of command and thus a source for a "prime directive." Second, in complex production systems individuals integrate psychologically the many different goals and objectives they experience daily by identifying with the person of the "commander." The commander comes to represent the organization as a whole. This is a principle of leadership. Third, when these conditions are absent, managers at all levels avoid acknowledging their accountability for their actions and instead blame the workers. Feeling unauthorized, management no longer takes responsibility for the risks of guiding and leading the enterprise. There is, consequently, a felt vacuum of authority throughout the organization.

This gives us a deeper insight into the experience of vulnerability. The technology at Ocean Reactor itself was demanding if not dangerous. Equally important, the plant's social system turned everyone into a suspect and a spy. Other people were threats. However, why would workers and managers facing a demanding technology create and reinforce a social system that increases rather than decreases the feeling of vulnerability? There is a simple rule operating here: Feeling vulnerable, people can transfer their attention from the dangerous object that creates the basic risks they experience to other people they believe they can control, communicate, or influence. They substitute the people they imagine they control for the risky technology (or market), which they cannot control.

Our penultimate meeting with our client was revealing. We met with Brad and other members of the management group as they assessed the dilemmas they faced in managing a set of procedures. We had prepared overhead slides to describe our key findings and some recommendations. We had peppered the deck of slides with some of our favorite Gary Larson cartoons. By matching certain cartoons to the contents of our presentation, we had always been able to get our previous clients to laugh and relax. This made it easier for us to talk about difficult issues, particularly at the beginning of the meeting. However, at this meeting, each cartoon was greeted with silence. The atmosphere was grim.

It is possible, of course, that joking about a nuclear power plant was taboo (like joking about cancer in the oncology unit of a university hospital). However, the people we interviewed and observed never appeared that grim or hopeless. They were proud of their efforts, though often frustrated by the organization. In retrospect, I believe that what I experienced among the managers was not resistance to humor itself (that is, to some funny "thing" or content) but resistance to the experience of having fun with one another. Humor, after all, is a link between individuals. If each manager around the table was dangerous to the others, one's laughter could then signify that one had let down one's guard. The enemy, so to speak, was not the technology but the other managers around the table.

The dynamics of the meeting showed the links between these feelings of vulnerability and abdication. As the end of the deliberations neared, it was not clear who had the authority to end the meeting. Brad tried to sum up the discussion several times but was interrupted by the Central Services manager and the Maintenance manager. They would not let him close the meeting. Curiously, though I had helped other management groups navigate through such quandaries in the past, this time I felt stuck. I then realized that, since Brad could not find the authority to take up his role as the meeting's conversation moderator, I could not find the authority to consult the group. Just as the organizational structure took authority from its employees, it had taken authority from me.

My co-consultant appeared similarly stymied and spoke up in a loud voice: "Now, who is responsible for doing what here?" At that moment, the chief operating officer, Jack, appeared. He stood, hugging the door frame of the conference room as if to communicate that he would observe the group's difficulties but would take no steps to join the group and wrestle with its difficulties. This moment revealed the links among vulnerability, authority, and abdication. The group faced difficulties in bringing its meeting to a close and in deciding what was to be done next. Because of the vacuum of authority, my client (Brad) felt both deskilled and vulnerable. The COO (Jack) reinforced the sense that he had abdicated by hovering at a distance. At that moment, all the members of the meeting were vulnerable, not to the COO's remonstrations, but to the increasing ineffectiveness of the group. At such moments, we turn on one another to identify and then box in the individuals we imagine are making us vulnerable, thus decreasing the group's effectiveness and intensifying everyone's vulnerability.

There has been no major incident or accident at Ocean Reactor. Although the organization burdens rather than supports its employees, the workers and supervisors are nonetheless personally committed to the plant's and the community's safety. Although many of the operators and technicians are angry with the organization, they nonetheless identify with their professions and with their craft (maintenance). Consequently, they can still perform successfully despite the political disorganization around them. They withdraw their mental and emotional energy from the organization and find their own personal reasons to work rationally, carefully, and effectively. But yet they work in a difficult climate—and, as one manager noted, the "next accident" can happen as a result of an operator's following procedures.

Abdication: Hierarchy versus Bureaucracy

Facing significant risks, leaders can abdicate their responsibilities by substituting a bureaucratic process for a functioning hierarchy. By contrast, in a well-functioning hierarchy the leader absorbs the primary risks of managing the enterprise and then delegates authority and accountability to others to accomplish the more limited but still complicated and important tasks. The leader in his or her role represents the organization as a whole and integrates the actions of its various divisions. This structure and this process facilitate teamwork. By contrast, when hierarchy is poorly defined or weakened, leaders who do not take up their leadership roles fully and do not manage the risks of the enterprise fully cannot delegate authority to others. Instead, they rely on "technical" fixes and disorganizing politics. They try to use technically developed procedures or rules as substitutes for roles, and they employ the political principle of checks and balances to orchestrate inter-divisional relationships. Checks and balances replace unity of command, rules replace roles, and politics ultimately drives out teamwork. We create a bureaucracy. This suggests that bureaucracy (particularly in high-risk settings) is usefully interpreted not as a rational form of work organization but as a *regressed form of hierarchy.* Facing high risks, feeling vulnerable in their roles, and unwilling to manage, leaders avoid their responsibility for guiding the enterprise. Instead, they abdicate to a system of checks and balances and a system of procedures.

Openness

The leaders of Ocean Reactor were vulnerable as a result of two processes. First, they faced an unpredictable technical environment. They depended on the plant's technology to protect workers and nearby residents from possible catastrophe. Second, they depended on their own subordinates to perform effectively, be vigilant, respond well in emergencies, and detect early signs of incipient failure. Unable or unwilling to face their vulnerability to technology and their dependence on subordinates, they built a system of rules that on the surface promised certainty but in fact increased the danger of accidents. Nonetheless, these rules played an important role in shaping the relationships between leaders and followers. Leaders could deny their dependence on their subordinates—they only had to follow the rules—while subordinates were burdened by an even greater sense of responsibility. Since the rule system was incomplete and was implemented through a system of checks and balances, leaders actually became more vulnerable to their subordinates, but could deny that they had become more dependent on them. The leaders built up a series of "social defenses" to contain their sense of vulnerability, while at the same time increasing their actual vulnerability. Far from developing a culture of openness to manage risk effectively, the leaders isolated themselves.

This suggests that we do not need to rid ourselves of hierarchy; rather, we need to "post-modernize" it. Although writers often contrast hierarchy with participative culture, well-functioning hierarchies are based deeply on the principle of delegation that, at bottom, stimulates and requires senior executives to share their leadership with their subordinates. When senior executives delegate leadership, they are lending their authority, never relinquishing it. This means that they remain deeply implicated in the workings of the organization so that they never abandon their subordinates to the mythical power of rules and procedures. In bureaucracies, however, leaders indeed withdraw. Unable to attenuate employees' sense of being at great risk, they paradoxically increase everyone's sense of vulnerability.

The post-modern environment brings greater risk, which may subvert hierarchy. We undermine the principle of accountability that hierarchy was designed to illuminate, and we dull it with the diffusion of accountability—with the bureaucratic process.

But is it possible to build a post-modern organization while reinforcing hierarchy? Doesn't hierarchy contradict a culture of openness? I suggest that the post-modern enterprise embraces hierarchy but enlivens it with feelings and passion. It strengthens hierarchy by personalizing it. Only the enlivened hierarchy—one in which superiors and subordinates can work across recognized authority boundaries while retaining their distinctive roles—can suppress bureaucracy.

5

Heroism

As people in post-modern organizations experience greater risk, they need heroes—individuals who act courageously and intelligently to solve difficult problems or create new opportunities. Yet, in just these moment they may create fantasy heroes—individuals who fend for themselves while actually punishing real heroes.

I have argued that passion and commitment enliven hierarchy. In situations of significant risk the enlivened hierarchy can, in turn, stimulate the courage and heroism we need to confront these risks. Committed to the core task of the enterprise, the hero steps outside his or her role (sometimes disobeying superiors) to save the organization from likely failure. But if heroes step out of their roles, do they arrogate the organization's authority rather than extend their own? Having enlivened hierarchy to contain our bureaucratic impulses, do we inherit the dangers of the undisciplined hero?

Imagine that an engineering company must have a working model of a new machine ready for an annual trade show. If it fails to do so, impatient investors will stop the machine's development; without their financing, the company will go bankrupt. An engineer, conscious of the deadline, decides to experiment with a new composite material. If he fails to weld this material to the heat-sensitive parts of the machine, he may damage a crucial mechanism. If he succeeds, he will be able to deliver a working model to the trade show. Believing that there is no time to get permission for such an experiment, he takes the risk, develops the material, creates the working model, and saves the company.

One might chuckle over such a Hollywood ending, but such minor and major acts of heroism happen every day. In the service of the task, the hero steps out of his role, fuses person with work, and (for the moment) dispenses psychologically with the organization as an entity. Our laughter at such endings in movies masks our ambivalence about the heroes. We need them, but in trying to save us they put us at great risk.

I once served on the board of a not-for profit organization that was in financial trouble. We were interviewing the "short list" of candidates for the executive director position, but all of us felt that "the fix was in." A man familiar to us all and deeply involved with the organization would clearly be hired. But when we met the only "stranger" candidate, half of the board was swept away by his character and presentation. He was direct, grounded, and focused. He stood before us as himself, with no intention of selling himself. I experienced the excitement his prospective hiring created for us. Unknown as he was, he felt like the "daring choice." Many of us harbored the fantasy that he would match our daring, heroic behavior with his own heroic actions—in other words, we felt that we could be heroes, and participate in his potential heroism, by hiring him. Ultimately, in what I considered an act of cowardice, the board hired the more familiar candidate. Others felt that our hero fantasies had been misguided and that we would be putting the organization at great risk. But who is to say that we adventurers were wrong? The new director succeeded, but perhaps our dark horse could have excited the organization's staff to reach for the stars.

We simultaneously crave and resist heroes who ask for our allegiance. This dilemma is resolved, in part, when people feel that a would-be hero, while distinctive, appears to be part of a cultural process of renewal and revitalization. One cannot but be struck by the large number of military and political heroes who emerged in the 1920s and the 1930s to build the state of Israel. It is not simply that extraordinary times created extraordinary people; rather, these heroes—Moshe Dayan, Shimon Peres, Yigall Alon, Golda Meir— were nourished by the widely shared dream of rebuilding a Jewish homeland while breaking from the culture of village Judaism that had once thrived in Eastern Europe. In other words, these heroes were participants in a cultural drama. This suggests that would-be heroes are less likely to succeed, and more likely to be suspected, when they are experienced as alone—when their heroic stance derives too much from personal ambitions rather from communal dreams and hopes.

These dynamics of heroism are particularly relevant to the postmodern organization. We need heroes in risky situations, and this is the basis of our yearning for leaders. But, since risky situations create substantial anxiety, we may choose to withdraw psychologically from the dangers we face and to seek out scapegoats who become, in our minds, the root causes of our anxiety. We are torn between yearning for heroic leaders and disavowing them completely. Because we feel passive, and therefore take little responsibility for our own actions and choices, it is easy to reject a failed leader as someone who was alien to us. Under these conditions, heroes risk feeling isolated. Such a stance confirms to them and us that they must stand alone, that their abilities are nourished entirely from the strength of their character. This stance, in turn, deepens their isolation.

Example: A Human Resources Department

I was consulting to the Human Resources Department of a factory responsible for making and shipping subassemblies of airplanes, which were then shipped to a sister plant for assembly. The Human Resources Department was accountable for the usual array of personnel programs: training shop-floor workers, teaching managers leadership skills, implementing various benefits programs, and so forth. However, the employees of this department were not entirely satisfied with the department's work. They wanted to develop and implement policies that were more directly linked to the problems that line managers dealt with directly from day to day. In response to the frequent and severe production bottlenecks that threatened the timely shipment of parts and thus threatened the company's ability to deliver aircraft to its customers when promised, there had emerged what the Human Resources managers called a "crisis culture"—a culture in which managers who solved a production crisis were heroes. This crisis culture was self-reinforcing, since it created few incentives for managers to learn to plan and coordinate their work more effectively. They were consequently unable to prevent production crises. Instead the company had developed the ritual of dubbing certain conference rooms "war rooms." As one Human Resources manager wryly noted, "you could get one of these rooms named after you if you solved a particularly severe production bottleneck." The Human Resources managers believed that this cultural problem lay at the heart of many of the problems the plant faced in improving its productivity.

Wondering how they could help reshape this dysfunctional culture, the Human Resources managers asked me to help them think through this issue. They and I soon discovered that we were enacting the very problem we were trying to understand. At several sessions, we made substantial progress; however, after I left, the group had second thoughts: Would this really lead anywhere. Where exactly were we going? How did we know our ideas would prove useful? Feeling their ambivalence, I became more aggressive, focusing their thinking on particular opportunities for action and identifying line managers who would cooperate with them. My aggressiveness backfired, and after one important meeting my contact person on the client team called to tell me that group members felt very doubtful that our joint efforts would succeed. They needed, he said, to meet by themselves to take a "pulse check."

What happened here? In retrospect it is clear that, feeling the Human Resources managers' growing ambivalence, I only doubled my efforts to save them—to be their hero—and in so doing I progressively isolated myself. By making their agenda my own agenda, I lost touch with their development as a group. This experience, I later suggested to them, reflected the culture of the company's approach to problem solving: people feel stuck; a hero emerges to save the group; the group loses its voice and becomes more dependent; the hero, feeling his isolation, redoubles his effort to save the group. If the hero fails, his failure is likely to be final, since people will now feel betrayed by his false promises. Under these conditions, fewer potential heroes are likely to step forward further; thus, the group's abilities to solve problems are stultified. This is the same process that has recently caused some leaders to withdraw from political and institutional life.

We cannot simply decry heroes or the heroic fantasy. Civilization's accomplishments depend deeply on the concept of heroism, and few people would willingly take up roles as self-abnegating leaders if they were not at first stimulated by their wish to perform heroic deeds, to achieve, to be noticed, to be recognized. Heroism is a fundamental component of human identity, and heroes can help even the more timid among us tact courageously. Rather than quash potential heroes, we should help them amplify our own cultural strivings. Just as we follow them, they should become part of us.

In order to understand this process in greater detail, let us examine the case of an oil refinery where, in facing risky conditions, workers and managers created a culture in which heroes were scapegoated.

Example: The Smalltown Oil Refinery

An oil refinery employing about 200 people and producing 50,000 barrels of gasoline a day was the dominant employer in a northwestern city. Situated on a plain with flat-topped mountains in the background, the refinery dominated part of the cityscape. The city's culture could be called "modern frontier." The blue-collar workers at the refinery came from families long native to the area; many of the financial and commercial managers had been transferred from elsewhere.

The refinery appeared orderly, with the large tanks, vats, and pipes laid out over acres of land. There were two control room structures, each a cross between an office building and a shack. "Indoor" workers sat in these buildings monitoring the flow and refining of oil, while "outdoor" workers toured the wide expanse of the yard, checking meters and valves while looking for dangers signs such as leaks and pockets of gas. The main office building, which stood at one end of the refinery, was unpretentiously furnished. A recently installed computer console gave the refinery's manager up-to-the-minute information on operations in all significant parts of the yard.

From telephone interviews my colleague and I had conducted before visiting the plant, we knew that the refinery was a profitable 40-year-old operation going through a slow process of modernization and development. Responding to a company-sponsored early retirement program three years before our visit, 25 percent of the workforce had left. The refinery had brought in some skilled operators from other parts of the company and some well-educated young people to fill the vacancies, so the overall educational level of the workforce had risen. In addition, at the time of our visit management was building a centralized control room using up-to-date computer graphics and electronic control systems to improve workers' ability to monitor and control plant conditions. Finally, George, the plant manager, who had come to the refinery five years before our visit, was working to improve a once-contentious labor-management relationship. The previous manager, who had once proudly proclaimed that "boss" spells "double SOB backwards," had little interest in working with the union to improve safety and working conditions. George, in contrast, routinely consulted the union president and had established a labor-management safety committee.

Despite these improvements the plant, was not functioning smoothly. There were significant tensions between members of the "combination unit" (the purpose of which was to separate crude oil into fractions of different weights) and members of the "condensation unit" (where the resulting fractions were refined). The workers particularly resented Gerry, a member of the condensation unit; they considered her hostile and aggressive. George was frustrated by the slow implementation of his safety reforms. The labor-management relationship, though better, still could be tense and disruptive at times. Finally, a year before, the refinery had experienced two severe fires. No one had been killed, but in the second fire several workers had narrowly escaped serious injury. After the second fire, George had asked Don, a company psychologist, to assess how stress might be affecting safety. In turn, Don had asked me to help him.

After studying both fires, a company audit team explained how each fire had been caused by a chain of successive events. No single event or person had been solely responsible. Before the first fire, operators shutting down the refinery for routine maintenance had been unaware of piping changes that had caused distillate to be pushed through an open valve and into the yard. As a result, the area around the pipe had smelled like gas. Some operators had noticed the distillate leaking from a pump but had not associated it with any evident safety problem. Others had assumed that the gassy smell was normal for a shutdown. Distillate had accumulated on the ground, and electrical sparks had ignited it. Thus, the stress of a shutdown, a valve left open, operators' ignorance of changes to the piping, and inattention to the signs of danger all conspired to create the fire. The fire illuminated a set of relationships among people, within the machinery, and between the people and the machinery which had coalesced to create the accident. Everything and nothing was to blame.

The Consultation Process

After talking with George (the manager), Don and I agreed to visit the refinery for two days to help workers and managers assess some of the issues that affected safety and organizational functioning. After conducting interviews with individual managers and workers, we met with three groups. The first group, the refinery's Health and Safety Committee, was composed of two managers and five union members. The second group was made up of workers from various categories who had been brought together during the consultation to discuss the relationships between operators and their assistants (called "controlmen"). The third group, composed of workers and supervisors from the "back end" and the "front end" of the refinery, was assembled to focus on the development and staffing of the soon-to-be-completed central control room.

At each meeting Don, George, and I sat around a conference table and spoke with between six and eight other individuals. We presented some general propositions about safety to the first group, stimulating them to examine when and why refinery workers behaved in an unsafe manner. The second group examined the refinery's chain of command, assessing whether its many levels made it difficult for individuals to feel accountable. The third group talked about the design of the centralized control room, looking at the links between control-room personnel and yard workers and between the back and front ends of the refinery. These conversations led to no immediate decisions; however, they helped raise awareness about safety, and they brought people from different units and levels together.

Although we touched upon a wide range of issues in the aforementioned meetings, I want to emphasize here how the culture of heroism contributed to the plant's dysfunction. Stories of the plant's heroes and villains provide insight into the role that heroes played in the Smalltown Oil Refinery's culture.

Everyone Is a Hero

The refinery was located in a part of the country where solitary heroes were celebrated in the folklore and where "frontier" values such as gun ownership and physical prowess were dominant. Frontier heroes believe in their invulnerability and value their independence Such heroes may fare well where they are in fact alone; however, when facing a complex technology that poses dangers to life and limb, people who imagine themselves to be heroes can needlessly increase the risks they and others face. By denying their dependence on others, they also deny the dangerous features of the technology. As the audits of the two fires at Smalltown showed, people in a refinery depend deeply on one another because each person monitors and controls an operation that affects all other operations. This is the hallmark of any continuous-process production system. Denying dependence increases the chance that accidents will happen.

To act safely and prevent accidents, individuals must be vigilant. This means that they must imagine that they are vulnerable to being hurt. By previewing the possible consequences of a dangerous situation in one's mind, one collaborates with others to take appropriate preventive action. In other words, people prevent accidents by imagining that they have already had them.

Clearly, vigilance is a complex activity. A person who becomes excessively preoccupied with potential accidents will be unable to work; moreover, such an individual's excessive anxiety is likely to infect others, disabling them too. (For example, workers who put up skyscrapers and walk the steel girders hundreds of feet above the ground shun novices who cannot keep their worries to themselves.) Thus, in order to act safely, workers in a dangerous setting must be aware without losing their ability to focus on their work. To strike this balance, the workers must avail themselves of the myth of the hero. They need to be somewhat heroic in order to be *appropriately* cautious.

Safety programs and guidelines play an important role here. As we saw in the case of Ocean Reactor (chapter 4), procedures play a critical role in helping people strike the balance between work and worry. They reduce the burdens of vigilance by helping people act safely without thinking excessively about the potential dangers that shape these procedures. Enacting the procedures without a great deal of conscious thought, people protect themselves without obsessively previewing the accidents that may hurt them. Free of excessive worry, they can focus on their work.

Smalltown's safety director believed that plant workers had failed to strike the appropriate balance between behaving heroically and behaving cautiously. He felt unable to educate them to behave safely or to enforce safety procedures. Reflecting on his ineffectiveness, he highlighted two seemingly contradictory processes. On one hand, he noted, workers in the plant often played the hero by taking shortcuts—for example, refusing to wear a safety belt when working over a pit. On the other hand, he noted, workers often employed laborious and apparently useless procedures, arguing "It's written that you have to do it this way" even in cases where the safety director found no evidence to support such an argument. Thus, the procedural system was split between dangerous shortcuts and senseless protocols. Using shortcuts, workers could pretend that they were invulnerable; using senseless protocols not connected to actual dangers, workers did not have to preview potential accidents. Thus, in each case workers denied the dangers confronting them. They could not apply procedures *intelligently*, with just enough conscious thinking to assess why they were acting in a particular way. Heroism stimulated mindlessness.

The Manager as Hero

Our relationship with the manager of the refinery also highlighted this culture of the hero. Although he sponsored the consultation and worked with us over the course of the two days, George communicated that he did not really need us and could, if he so desired, remain untouched by our work. Sitting at the conference table, arms folded, with the three different groups, he never once lifted his pencil to take notes or jot things down, as if to communicate that he either already knew or would surely remember everything being said. Similarly, after the first day he said to me "It's useful to have the other people here learn about these issues," as if to suggest that he had learned nothing. When I reminded him that he had been surprised by a discussion of the foreman's role in ensuring safety, he agreed, like a hero reluctant to acknowledge that he could profit from depending on others.

Yet while projecting invulnerability—his ability to avoid being influenced by us—George periodically expressed enormous frustration. He could not imagine how, despite any insights he might obtain during the meetings, he could actually improve safety. In a moment of frustration, he said "I guess all I can do is go out there and really start to walk around, take people on tours with me, show them what is dangerous, why this ladder can't be left in the middle of the yard when it snows." In other words, he could not imagine working *through* his organization—leveraging his efforts through others. Instead, he would be the hero, taking workers on his tours and showing them, by example, what it meant to be safe. This idea in itself was not wrong; however, said in frustration, it reflected George's sense of isolation and his compensatory fantasy that he could act heroically. As the hero, he had nothing to learn, but as a loner, as someone who could not collaborate, he could not act effectively.

The Pair as Hero

On the first morning of the consultation, George, the members of the Health and Safety Committee, and a few other high-level supervisors examined obstacles to improving safety at the refinery. Describing the process of bringing suggestions from workers to management, Mike, a union representative on the committee, noted that he took workers' ideas to managers without involving or informing the foremen. I suggested that this could backfire because foremen might feel that health and safety programs were designed to undermine their authority, and they might not cooperate. This statement seemed to create discomfort. People were silent, then George said "Well, I don't know if people agree with that." Feeling the anxiety, I said "People are not saying all that they are thinking." Then Jim, the assistant manager, got up and said "Whew, I guess it's time to take a break." Later Jim noted that this had been his most important learning of the day.

Looking back, I suggest that the dynamics of the Health and Safety Committee had helped create a fantasy among the members of the committee that George, with a few cooperative union people such as Mike, could circumvent the institutional matrix of the refinery—the historically complex union-management relationship and the refinery's complex chain of command—and create a safe, happy, productive place to work. Throughout the morning Don and I were struck by the apparent eagerness of Mike—the most active union member on the committee—to defend the plant. Mike, an intense young man, sat directly opposite of George, and as the morning's discussion progressed it appeared that George and Mike represented what Wilfred Bion calls the "pairing fantasy"—the wish that two special people can help a group overcome obstacles while freeing the others from the difficult work.[1] My statement about Mike's neglecting the fore-

1. Wilfred Bion, *Experiences in Groups* (Basic Books, 1959).

men threatened to undermine this fantasy. Pointing the participants back to the messy world of disgruntled foremen, I suggested that the Health and Safety Committee, despite the fantasy it enacted and contained, could not magically and heroically transform the refinery. Other people could undermine its efforts.

The Anti-Hero

Gerry, who worked in the condensation unit (Unit 2), played the peculiar role of the anti-hero. People projected the dark side of heroism onto her. Everyone described her as obstinate, as difficult to work with, and as "someone who always thinks she's right." The condensation unit was regarded as the most troublesome unit at the refinery, and people believed that Gerry's character was a factor in this. Gerry was often contrasted with Dianne, a worker in the combination unit (Unit 1) who held picnics for co-workers at her home and who was sometimes affectionately called "Princess Di." Toward the end of our consultation, one member of Unit 2 asked to see Don (the company psychologist) privately to discuss the trouble he and others were having with Gerry. People were wary of her and seemed to resent the ways in which she was different. She lived alone, could fix cars, knew the martial arts, and was separated from a man who had abused her.

Interviewing Gerry, I found her boyish, tough-looking, lively, feisty, demanding, committed to productive work, and unhappy with the laziness and inattention she observed around her. Describing the first fire, which occurred on her shift, she expressed the feeling that the workers and managers had known that they were using "dirty charge" but had decided to forget about it and "pretend that they didn't have a problem." At the second of the three group discussions, she took the role of the fighter, arguing that the controlmen ought to be more accountable for their work. Her affect was vital, and I felt strongly that she wanted to connect to the group and contribute to the discussion.

To her co-workers Gerry represented the negative side of heroism. By describing her as aggressive and obstinate, they re-framed her heroic characteristics (independence, mastery of martial arts) as signs of excessive willfulness and an inability to get along and cooperate. People were using Gerry as a symbolic repository for their negative images of the hero as a dangerous or uncontrollable person while re-taining the positive images for themselves. They were reserving the right to take heroic shortcuts without holding themselves account-able for the difficulties heroes can create for others.

Gerry suffered significantly because she was isolated and dis-trusted. Reflecting on the social process of the refinery, she noted: "Paybacks are a bitch here, and they last forever. A person can make life absolutely hell out here. If you ever let anyone see that anything bothered you, they would pick at that." To be safe from attacks by other people, a person with any amount of power had to appear in-vulnerable. Gerry was saying that *the negative parts of the hero role had been thrust upon her.* If she were to act vulnerable, people would discover her weak points and attack her.

Gerry's role as the anti-hero may have contributed to the acci-dent in the condensation unit. On the night of the fire, a control-man who officially worked under Gerry's direction had openly defied an instruction she had given him. The audit did not iden-tify this as the cause of the accident but Don's and my hypothesis points to a plausible indirect connection. By defying Gerry in public, the controlman had created a psychodrama in which the group had symbolically destroyed the bad and unreliable Gerry. Feeling safe, they became less vigilant and created the conditions for a fire.

The Would-Be Hero as Scapegoat

Bill, a controlman's helper who had recently joined the refinery as a member of the "good" combination unit, was another victim of the hero system. In the second fire, Bill rushed toward the flames just after a propane explosion to shut off a valve. However, his experi-ence as a hero was to be short-lived.

The day before the fire, Bill had volunteered to climb up a steel structure to open a valve. However, he and the other two operators he had been assisting had failed to close a bleeder that had to be lined up with the valve. While officially being supervised by the op-erator standing below, it had been Bill's responsibility to check if the bleeder and the valve were lined up. This open bleeder was the proximate cause of the fire, and after a careful investigation, man-agement sent Bill a letter of reprimand.

Toward the end of the second day of our consultation, Bill's supervisor, Tom, approached Don and asked if he would see Bill. Tom noted that Bill, having received his reprimand, was "really hurting." Bill's teammates had written a letter to management asking that the reprimand be withdrawn. Management had not backed down, and the letter of support from the unit had done little to lift Bill's spirits. I asked Don if I could join him in the interview with Bill, and he agreed.

Several hours later Tom brought Bill to an office in the main suite, gently pushing him by one elbow much as one guides a child or an invalid. Bill sat down and began recounting the accident and its aftermath.

After describing the accident in some detail, Bill remarked on how hard it was to be a hero one day and a villain the next. He said how badly he felt the next day when people, unaware of his role in the accident, congratulated him for his courageous behavior. He noted how horrible he felt whenever he passed a particular teammate who had almost been killed in the fire. He said he had once held a job as a pipefitter in another factory where "when you f***ed up, they beat you up and sent you down the road."

At first glance this discussion creates the impression of a depressed and guilty man who has been punished by his superiors and is punishing himself. However, four other parts of the conversation paint a more complex picture. First, Bill's face and voice were animated, as if he were describing an exciting sports event or movie. Highlighting the initiative he took to open the valve the day before and then describing his courageous behavior during the accident, he appeared to be telling us "You should have been there." Second, Bill described his teammates' letter of support contemptuously. Saying that he didn't care about "that little letter," he criticized the first draft for being insufficiently diplomatic toward top management. Third, testing for depression, we asked Bill if he was having trouble sleeping or was waking up early; he said "No." "How about eating?" we inquired. "I have to lose some weight," he replied. Fourth, we were unable to say anything helpful to Bill. "Would it help talking to the man you almost killed?" we asked. He answered "No." Perhaps he did not like all the care he was getting and would rather be beaten up as he was when employed as a pipefitter, we suggested. No, he didn't think that was it. We asked why he thought he was solely responsible. "Well, I opened the valve," he replied. Unable to say anything useful to him, we began to feel increasingly helpless. As the conversation wound down, Bill said, somewhat contemptuously: "Well, you guys are giving me all these theoretical ideas. I thought you were going to help me."

Far from being depressed and guilty, Bill was ashamed of his failure and enraged at his subsequent humiliation. To get back at the plant community, which was sophisticated enough to try and help him after it had punished him, he refused to be helped. In this way he transferred his feelings of helplessness back onto the plant community and onto us. He did not want us to help him; he wanted us to feel helpless.

The Dance of Projection

Bill and the plant were engaged in a complex dance of projection. The plant community, anxious to control its own sense of vulnerability after the accident, scapegoated Bill by reprimanding him. He had indeed been partly responsible for the fire, and he had been careless. But one operator had been supervising him, and another had been working along with him. More important, management had been pushing the employees to work quickly so that the refinery could be restarted without delay. Bill's supervisor, Tom, who brought him to his appointment with us, told us that he worried that he had pushed the people too hard before the accident.

Because Bill was easily humiliated (a reflection of the sense of omnipotence that led him to act heroically, if sometimes carelessly), he refused to be scapegoated. Instead, by refusing to be helped he put his own sense of helplessness back into the system. Anxious to protect themselves from feeling vulnerable, other members of the plant community now felt powerless to help Bill. Just as social splits distributed feelings of helplessness between the "good" and the "bad" unit, Bill had turned feelings of helplessness into a "hot potato."

In making Don and me feel helpless, Bill brought us to the edge of such feelings as despair, anger, and contempt. We disliked him for having made us helpless, and we disliked ourselves for failing. I suggest that similar feelings shaped the unconscious experiences of people working at the refinery. Feeling vulnerable in a dangerous situation and unable or unwilling to trust the "heroes" around them, they developed feelings of contempt and anger for social scapegoats such as Gerry, Unit 2, or the troublemakers that once populated Unit 1 in order to control their own feelings of vulnerability.

Bill was singled out in part because of his capacity to act heroically. The young controlman's helper had acted impulsively in opening the valve and had acted truly heroically during the accident. Speaking rationally, one might say that in order to develop self-discipline he had to be disciplined. Speaking irrationally, one might say that, as a newcomer, he was an easy projective target for people's anxiety that heroes were uncontrollable, too independent, and therefore dangerous. The hero in him had to be tamed so that it could be manifested in subtler ways that would be acceptable to the plant's culture—for example, violating a procedure or keeping to himself. He had been reprimanded, not because he had caused an accident (much evidence suggests that he was not solely to blame), but *because he was a hero.*

When workers project their feelings of vulnerability onto scapegoats and anti-heroes, they feel safe without paying sufficient attention to signs of danger. More important, they do not simply become less vigilant. Rather, *they turn their vigilance inward*, away from the technology and the artifacts of production and toward the social system. They pay undue attention to the defensive relationships they have constructed with one another, isolating anti-heroes such as Gerry and constraining their own expression of vulnerability for fear of "paybacks." The social defense system itself becomes the focus of attention. As people pay undue attention to their relationships and too little attention to the technology, they create rather than contain danger.

The Organization and the Hero

Let us return to the links between the heroes and the organizations in which they work. Because an oil refinery is a dangerous place to work, it provides us with an interesting model for understanding how a post-modern organization functions when its members face high levels of marketplace risk. As people become preoccupied with the survival of the organization or of their divisions, how do they cope as individuals and as a group? For example, at the aircraft factory described above, the culture of heroism flourished just at a time when people began asking "In light of the competitive pressures we face, can the company survive?" Overcoming bottlenecks became the symbol of saving the organization. But, as we have seen, it also undermined the capacity of people to collaborate when collaboration was most urgently needed.

Organizations are designed to reduce their members' vulnerability and exposure. However, if an organization appears to be at too great a risk, its members will psychologically detach themselves from the organization and its risks by imagining that they are heroes. In becoming heroes, they act out the fantasy that they are self-sufficient. On the other hand, they also grow wary of individuals they suspect of masquerading as heroes—people who, like false messiahs, threaten to destroy the organization. They transform unknowable risks into the dangers that particular people or groups can create. In each case they create the fantasy that they are now invulnerable—that they are protected from danger either because they are heroes or because they have isolated the dangerous would-be heroes.

When the hero complex dominates, people feel invulnerable with respect to the objective dangers; however, they feel very vulnerable to paybacks and pressures from co-workers. When the hero complex is attenuated (it cannot be and should never be eliminated), people become open to one another and, through their good work, feel less threatened by the objective danger.

Engaging Our Heroes

The post-modern organization animates the role with the qualities of the person. By stepping out of his or her role, the hero culminates this process. But this step is developmental only when breaking the role boundary brings the hero close to the core tasks of the enterprise so that he emerges from the protective shadow of the role to face the task, the work, directly.

This will happen only if the task itself is valued and shared by all. Engaging our heroes means building and sharing a vision of the enterprise, a sense of its purpose, that supports (if only temporarily) the sense of identity of a hero or a non-hero. This vision helps people address some never-to-be-fully-answered questions: What is the "good" professional? What is the moral meaning of work? What does it mean to offer my services? How does good design give meaning to objects? When heroes and others share this vision, they can engage one another and stimulate more heroism, more action, and more planning. The American labor movement, for example, produced large numbers of heroes, from leaders like Walter and Victor Reuther to nameless heroes who took physical risks to protect their dignity and their identity as citizens. All shared a moral vision of what it meant to be a worker. Similarly, two of our great American heroes, Abraham Lincoln and Robert E. Lee, were able to take up their roles because each experienced his stance as connected to and nourished by a wider vision: for Lincoln, the constitution; for Lee, the South.

Organizations are not social movements, but they too provide meaning and help people shape their identities as competent workers, good professionals, and responsible managers. If the post-modern organization is to engage its heroes, it too needs a shared purpose— not one that is artificially constructed ("our mission is to . . ."), but one that grows out of the work people do and the customers they serve. To build such a shared purpose, members must become more open and vulnerable to one another. Only in exploring who they are with one another can they discover what they share and what they hope for.

6

Toward a New Sensibility

In chapter 5 I suggested that we can draw upon a hero's courage if we all acknowledge our dependency on one another—if we don't pretend that each us of is a hero, invulnerable to injury. We need instead to work in a "culture of openness" in which, through our psychological presence to one another, we acknowledge the centrality of our relationships. Indeed, throughout this book I have suggested that without such a culture the post-modern enterprise is likely to fail. But I have also shown how difficult it is to create such an organizational culture when our individual and collective responses to risk and anxiety pull us apart instead of bringing us together. I have suggested that when people share a purpose in a work setting they can overcome these difficulties. But is this sufficient? Organizations can help people use a shared purpose to make moral meaning of their activities, but can they provide the emotional and conceptual ground for having meaning? An organization, after all, is not a religious institution. Its primary purpose is neither to educate nor to inspire. In light of these difficulties, what confidence do we have that we can indeed build such an organizational culture? A historical analogy is helpful here.

The capitalist revolution, Weber argued, thundered through Europe because the Reformation had established a culture receptive to capitalistic practices. The Protestant emphasis on each individual's relationship to God established the foundation for entrepreneurship, Weber asserted. The Calvinist conception of grace—that a person likely to be saved was one who already appeared to be "elected"—stimulated ambition and planning. The Protestant conception of frugality, or its obverse, its hatred of decadence and ostentatious behavior, laid the groundwork for the capitalistic emphasis on saving. Capitalism as an arrangement of economic practices could thrive only because a supporting culture nourished it. As an instrument for creating wealth, the market could not create moral meaning. Instead, said Weber, moral meaning was infused from without.

I believe that the same holds true for the post-modern organization. Organizations cannot lift themselves up culturally and morally by their bootstraps. People will not tolerate the anxieties associated with their being open and vulnerable simply because the success of the enterprise in which they work depends on their doing so. A person's relationship to an enterprise, particularly today, is too ephemeral to be the object of such commitment. Yet people will tolerate these anxieties because the culture of the post-industrial society predisposes them to do so. *They will attach moral meaning to acknowledging their interdependence if the wider culture makes such behavior and sentiments morally meaningful.*

This leads us to a more primary question: What is the evidence that the wider culture values the feelings of interdependence and the behaviors associated with bringing these feelings about? An individual's relationship to authority is telling here. When people feel dependent on authority, they suppress their awareness of their relationship to others by experiencing primarily their relationship to authority. By developing a fantasy of their special relationship to authority (either as the perfect subordinate or as the perfect rebel), they develop the spurious belief that they are not dependent on others.

There are ample indications that a new culture of authority has been emerging over the last three decades, however. Although Americans have always been resolutely democratic in their political traditions, they have in the past relied deeply on strict authority relationships in their daily practices. Children did not address adults by their first names, dressed differently from adults, and were prized for their obedience. Workers and managers wore different clothes, ate in separate cafeterias, and parked their cars in different parts of the lot. Women faced limited career prospects, took up support roles in the office, and, as wives, were expected to subordinate their wishes and desires to their husbands. Obviously, these cultural practices have been deeply challenged. Increasingly, people expect to negotiate the limits of their own and others' authority. In so doing they deepen their own sense of personal authority, their right to define the scope of their actions, the breadth of their vision, and the network of relationships in which they are embedded. They do this not as rebels, for a person can rebel only when facing an absolute constraint, but as participants in creating a shared reality. This suggests, of course, that people are less likely to submit passively to authority or to rebel compulsively against it. It is in this context that people become more aware of the group life around them, the team at work, and the family as a "system." In other words, they experience interdependence more deeply. This deeper sense of interdependence, accompanied as it is by a new relationships to authority, is the new sensibility of the post-industrial age.

There are other indications of such a new sensibility. Until the 1960s people were committed to a "linear" conception of the life course. One went to school, got a job, got married, raised children, advanced as far as one could in one's chosen career, retired, and died. Although this life course was not available to all (in particular, relatively few women had complete access to it), it was considered normative. Today we no longer rely on such a standard image of what it means to pass through life. The linear conception has been replaced by a developmental one. We expect to go through periods of crisis and renewal, to change careers, divorce, return to school, renew relationships with loved ones, and so on. We make ourselves increasingly open to our own experiences. Rather than suppress unhappiness or desire, we allow ourselves to be made aware of our goals, fulfilled or unfulfilled. We are unexpectedly touched by others—by a child who evokes new feelings of spontaneity, by the grief of a friend, by the contribution of a once-unnoticed colleague. By attaching moral meaning to being open in this way, we deepen our sense of interdependence.

To be sure, there are counter-tendencies. The quest for political absolutes, the worship of celebrity, the superficiality of revolving relationships, and the hatred of outsiders all point to a sensibility that narrows the range of others we consider important. These counter-tendencies are not simply expressions of the culture of individualism; they go beyond it to a culture of estrangement. In this sense it might be said that in the transition to a post-industrial society the new sensibility meets its shadow, so that we face not the old dichotomies of tyranny versus freedom or individualism versus collectivism but rather a dichotomy of the sense of community versus the experience of estrangement. Indeed, this new duality defines well the psychodynamics of today's organization. As we have seen throughout this book, the new conditions of work simultaneously pull us toward interdependence while pushing us toward estrangement. This is the new dialectic of the post-industrial age.

Depth, Breadth, and Discovery

The new sensibility rests on three interrelated ways of experiencing the self.

The first of these is experiencing the self in *depth*. A person has many levels of awareness about his or her own experience—some conscious, some accessible to consciousness, and some unconscious. When experiencing in depth, we use our feelings to uncover the reasons for our actions—reasons that often lie out of awareness. We experience our own experience more deeply.

The second is experiencing the self in *breadth*. A person's identity emerges from the widest set of relationships in which his or her life is embedded. The self is a social self. When thinking in breadth, we realize that our experiences are the echoes of other individuals' experiences, and that what we feel can represent truths about the system of relationships that surround us.

Third, through discovery the self evolves over the life span. A self is shaped by the its own discoveries—its nature changes. Hence, our conclusions are only hypotheses, and the meaning of an events is always provisional.

Each of these elements of the post-modern self helps us to become more open to one another. To be aware in depth means that my experience of another person is not self-evident to me. I respond fruitfully to the other person when I become more aware of the quality of my own awareness. Similarly, to be aware in breadth is to find my own experiences in others' experiences and theirs in mine. And when I am aware of my evolving self, I know that another to whom I was impervious may now touch me. Through each of these orientations I become more open and vulnerable to others.

The post-modern organization opens a social space in which we can take up these orientations and thus find a new sense of "being at work." Consider the following example.

Example: A Biomedical Group

I was facilitating a strategy meeting of a biomedical research group to help members plan their activities for the coming five years. I felt the work was going well; members had worked in small groups examining particular research areas and were now meeting in a plenary session to review what each group had discussed. As I facilitated a conversation, one researcher, Jack, a man in his early forties, rose and said to me forcefully: "I don't know if this is my own thing, perhaps my colleagues can help me here, but I think, you are talking entirely too much. You are here not to discuss your thoughts but to help us discuss ours."

I was, at first, taken aback. However, after thinking about it for a moment, I replied that what Jack had said made some sense. I realized that in fact I had stopped facilitating a conversation and had become a participant in it, with my own points to prove. Subsequently I focused on facilitating the session. By getting out of the way, I created space for members of the group to take a more active role in the meeting and to come to grips with their low self-esteem.

Jack's forcefulness suggested that he was talking from the heart, from his passions, and not simply being angry or competitive. He communicated to me and others the stakes he felt in the conversation. His phrase "I don't know if this is my own thing, perhaps my colleagues can help me here" invited responses and criticism. While I certainly felt criticized, I also felt challenged—Jack's forcefulness, combined with the risk he was taking, made me open to him rather than retreat in shame or petulance. Finally, reflecting on the conceit that had driven me to take center stage, I became vulnerable to myself.

In retrospect, I believe that I had taken center stage at this session not simply to star, but to inure myself to the feelings of frustration and helplessness the participants were beginning to express. Resisting their experience, I became part of the very psychosocial field that had been the object of my consultation.

Jack's stance was shaped by what we can call "feelings in depth" and "feelings in breadth." His forcefulness made evident his commitments and passions, his reference to his colleagues made evident his awareness that others might be having different experiences, and his challenge to me revealed his wish to collaborate. My own personal response, to explore my own behavior, mirrored the way in which Jack had opened himself and made himself vulnerable.

In my consultation to many organizations over the last two decades, I have become aware of this emerging "new sensibility" that is reshaping how people take up their roles. Like Jack, people at times can mobilize their own personal authority, their forcefulness, to collaborate more deeply with one another. Others, when not embarrassed or angered, can then speak from the heart as well. When this happens people become more aware of the difference experiences that shape any moment of interaction. A sense of interdependence thus grows.

Example: A National Foundation

A consultant frequently wrestles with the challenge of trying to understand his or her own experience in depth and breadth. Consider the following. I was asked to consult with a national foundation as it geared up to give sizable grants of money to states willing to develop innovative family-preservation programs. The purpose of the programs was to prevent the needless placement of children in foster care (particularly community homes) and, where placement was necessary, to shorten the time children spent separated from their families. The foundation's staff believed that the structure of social services made it difficult for public and private agencies to provide integrated services. Health care, home care, foster care, family therapy, welfare, and employment training were all provided and funded through different programs. The staff had a vision of a system in which one case manager would oversee the delivery of all social services to a family in need.

To help launch this initiative the foundation awarded planning grants to six states, asking them to develop a plan for creating a model of an integrated, family-preserving social service system. At the end of the planning process, the foundation sponsored a two-and-a-half-day planning conference at which representatives of the states were to review the major issues and themes of family preservation, review the foundation's guidelines for applying for the grants to undertake the actual social service reform efforts, and spend time preparing their applications for foundation support. The foundation wished to fund all six states, but was aware that one state lacked the commitment and leadership to develop a good plan. I was asked to help facilitate the conference.

The planning conference was designed to provide opportunities for people from the different states to talk with one another, for the conference's membership as a whole to consider the impact of state-local relationships on social service restructuring, and for the foundation to explain its philosophy of integrating social services. Seventy people, representing a wide range of roles in social service delivery in all six states, attended.

It is was a complex conference. People appeared inhibited and tense and seemed unresponsive to the tasks I set before them; they reluctantly participated in various subgroup discussions. Some appeared to be angry at me, at my facilitation, at my role, at my presence. I felt increasingly grim and isolated, and I doubted my competence. To be sure, large group meetings often create barriers to conversation, and many participants who occupied lower levels of authority in their state agencies may have been too anxious to talk.

In one curious event, the participants assessed how they should spend their free time after the first afternoon session. Like a slip of the tongue, this apparently trivial discussion exposed the depth and breadth of people's feelings about the work they did with children and families.

Joanne, a member of the foundation's staff, asked the other participants if they wanted to take part in karaoke that evening. The staff had secured an entertainer who had karaoke equipment, but if there was no interest, Joanne said, she would simply cancel the event. In a show of hands, only five people signaled that they wanted to participate. Joanne said she would cancel. A subdued sigh of regret then swept through the conference. Joanne once again called for a show of hands, and once again only five people offered to participate. Fifteen minutes later, Joanne reported to the conference staff that she had been "lobbied" in the women's restroom to retain the karaoke entertainment, and after conferring with us she did so. Forty people attended that evening and had a great time, and most stayed until the very end of the night.

One might imagine that many people were afraid of looking silly while singing old songs in front of their colleagues. Yet each time Joanne canceled the event many protested, both by sighing in the meeting room and by lobbying Joanne in the ladies' room—and more than a third of the participants ultimately attended the karaoke event. It makes more sense to say that many participants, despite their wishes to join in the singing, did not want to identify themselves as people eager to participate in something that was simply fun. In others words, if the opportunity were sanctioned, they would risk looking silly singing songs, but they did not want to risk revealing themselves as people who liked to do something silly. Why should this be?

It seems evident that the context for the conference made silly activities appear inappropriate, if not sacrilegious. Facing excessive caseloads, welfare workers often failed to help families while children suffered needlessly. Thus, singing at a karaoke event would be like dancing at a funeral. Moreover, many caseworkers undoubtedly felt implicated in the suffering of the children they were supposed to care for. They felt that they did not deserve to have fun.

The relationship between the foundation and the states played an important role too. Throughout the planning process, the foundation's staffers were very much preoccupied with whether or not the state personnel "got it"—that is, whether they understood the vision of child welfare services that the foundation wanted to support. I often felt that, by classifying people into those who got it and those who didn't, the foundation's managers and officers were distancing themselves from the pain embedded in the child welfare system. Children were suffering, but not because some recalcitrant workers failed to "get" the foundation's visions. Indeed, Joanne's hesitation in offering karaoke—she talked about canceling it just as she was offering it—felt stingy and withholding to me. In asking aggressively for a show of hands, Joanne appeared to be testing the members, as if asking "Do you think it is right for you to enjoy yourselves? If yes, raise your hand." Perhaps that is why the participants were stingy in their response.

This explanation helped me understand my experience, not simply as a product of who I was, but as the experience of someone whose feelings and awareness belonged to the system I was part of. As a facilitator of the conference, I had struggled throughout the plenary session to engage people, to create a context for lively discussion, but I felt powerless to do so. Instead, I too felt grim, constricted, inhibited, and depressed. I could not fathom my failure and apparent powerlessness. Reflecting on this, I came to understand in a very personal way the dynamic of helplessness that everyone participating in the child welfare system has experienced. Helplessness, I thought, could be expressed in many ways. A child feeling helpless might respond with rage, an older or disabled adult with passivity. But in this case I felt neither rage nor passivity but constriction and grimness. Since everyone felt victimized, I could not relax into my helplessness, nor could I feel "rageful" at anyone. There was simply no energy left in the system either to support me or to withhold support. Finally, this experience of grimness gave me a deeper understanding of why social service reform is so difficult today. The terrain of feeling and thinking has been so drastically narrowed that there is very little space for creativity and excitement.

This example provides four insights into the new sensibility.

First, participants in the session re-enacted their working relationships within the social services system by transferring critical feelings onto particular events and individuals (such as Joanne and me). The seemingly trivial karaoke event became a "critical incident" that exposed how people related to one another as a result of their shared relationship to the system of family services and foster care.

Second, to take up my role as a consultant I had to think in breadth. Foundation managers, conference participants, and I were linked by the feelings that undergirded and gave meaning to the work we tried to accomplish together. Feelings of constriction and inhibition were signals of the tasks and constraints we all faced in helping provide foster care for children. We do not have to look far to "see" the system; we reproduce it in its essentials from moment to moment.

Third, to take up my own role I had to understand my experience in depth. Upon feeling defeated and isolated, one can draw many conclusions—for example, one can say to oneself "That other person is impossible," or "I am incompetent," or "I have so few resources and time, " or "We are all victims of powerful forces." A single thought provides a partial and therefore superficial explanation for one's experience. Taken separately, each thought springs readily to mind, and becomes a rationalization, a cover for the other thoughts. It is the combination of all these thoughts that provides the deeper insight. For example, I could have given vent to feelings of depression by blaming myself for my failure to spark discussion. Feeling depressed, I could then at least have felt that I had paid the price for my failure. But in doing so I would have denied the reality of the participants' pain. Similarly, feeling victimized, I could have blamed the foundation for setting me up in an impossible task. But then I would have been denying the grandiosity I had mobilized to take up such a role when people were patently afraid and lonely. (I could have seen this at the very beginning of the conference had I not been caught up in my hero fantasies.) Each thought is true but partial, and therefore when taken alone each covers up all the others. To think in depth we must entertain all these thoughts simultaneously, so that we can see, taste, and smell the piece of reality each thought represents.

Finally, every thought is a hypothesis, and as we share it with others we can see more complexities, more nuances. We don't increase our knowledge so much as we deepen our appreciation. As we discover more meanings the experience is enriched, but the discovery process is always incomplete. I talked at length about this with Fred, the man who managed the project for the foundation. He too had felt displaced by the conference. At first he attributed this to me, but he then agreed that I had appeared increasingly deflated over the course of the conference. We did not resolve our differing feelings, we simply held them. Interestingly, six months later, after Fred facilitated a similar conference of caseworkers, he appeared deflated, though I thought the conference had gone well. I reminded him of my experience and suggested that the crisis of child welfare may have mobilized in each of us hero fantasies about how we could save the system and ultimately save children.

Indeed, as I write this text I can appreciate how Fred's and my system-saving fantasies may parallel a caseworker's wish to save a child. If this is so, our experience sheds light on the complexity of the child-saving fantasy. If caseworkers are brutally realistic, if they say "I cannot save children, that's it," they may become cynical. But if caseworkers persist in believing in the heroic impact of their personal efforts they are likely to feel despair.

Conclusion

A psychodynamically oriented consultant learns to think in breadth and depth, although his own limits, defenses, and conceits mean that he never "gets it right"—failure is a precondition for becoming aware. I don't mean to glorify the consultant here either. He faces special obligations and responsibilities. To be successful in his role, he must grapple with the new sensibility. But I believe that increasingly people are taking up their work roles in the context of this new sensibility. In the following chapter I present an example of how the new sensibility is made manifest in the day-to-day relationships people face at work.

7

Resentment and Gratitude

I have argued that a new sensibility is emerging which helps people experience their interdependence more deeply. Yet it is also evident that the transition to a post-industrial society fragments our relationships. In particular, the transition creates much resentment.[1] Those who lose status resent those who have gained it; those who have gained it resent the charge that they have not earned it. Students resent submitting to the authority of teachers, who appear victimized themselves. Older people who worked hard to develop their skills resent young people who dismiss their knowledge as obsolete. Young people, eager to advance, resent apparently unproductive older people who block their mobility. Wives resent husbands who can no longer support their families; husbands resent wives who no longer respect them or who must support them. Building new institutions, social networks, and relationships to and with authority is profoundly difficult in a society that witnesses the betrayal of so many expectations and promises. Social and psychological dislocation make it doubly hard for people to collaborate.

In the electronics factory I described in the introduction to this book, the workers on the plant floor resented their supervisors greatly for past mistreatment. This resentment made it difficult for workers to collaborate with supervisors to construct a culture in which workers would have more authority on the plant floor. The supervisors resented the abuse they were given—after all, they had been hired to take up the role of overseer and disciplinarian because

1. Resentment has long been studied as social force and process in society. Here I add to the discussion by focusing on its psychological implications and by demonstrating how if affects organizations.

this is what they had to do. The two groups could not collaborate in building a new working relationship.

Resentment, derived in the first instance from actual experience, is also fueled by the fantasies and feelings we bring to experience. I once consulted to the research division of a pharmaceutical company. There, Ira, a vice-president in charge of developing a drug and bringing it to market quickly, acted as if his group's work represented the division's highest priority. He often refused to compromise when resources had to be shared among departments and product groups. He spoke against Paul, the president; he was wary of most efforts to "bring the top team together." Acting as if he were being victimized and abused, Ira resented all efforts to make him submit to group discipline. Eventually, to his great surprise, Paul fired him. Apparently Ira had not taken the measure of his defiance, though it was very disruptive to others. Since his misreading was so dramatic, it is likely that he saw the situation—an obdurate president, his star status, and others' unjustified desire for his resources—through the lens of his inner resentments, derived perhaps from the experiences of his early life. He brought forward the resentment that lay within him.

Indeed, authority relations are crucial in such a case. Authority relations are the family's crucible. Our tendency to both resent others and feel grateful toward them is based on the dynamics of domination and submission in our families of origin. Did we experience our parents as tyrannical? Did they let our siblings dominate us? Could we find our own voices? In submitting to our parents did we gain protection and nurture, and in following our siblings did we learn from their experience? These universal experiences leave a residue of envy and resentment in all of us; however, we can contain these feelings, and even diminish their impact, as experience teaches us that, in the main, our realistic efforts bring us rewards. But when social dislocation intensifies, our actual failures rekindle the feelings of resentment and envy we had once contained.

The antidote to resentment is gratitude: the conviction that, despite our disappointments, others have contributed to our lives, and that we are the better for it. Melanie Klein suggests that we overcome our resentments when, instead of splitting off our bad experiences from our good ones, we begin to see that ultimately each is implicated in the other.[2] At bottom, gratitude stems from the existential insight that, despite the certainty of death, we are grateful for having been offered life.

This means that feelings of gratitude do not stem only from pleasant experiences. A student, for example, will feel grateful toward his mentor even if (and often because) the mentor insists on discipline and perfection. The student is grateful that the mentor takes him seriously enough to commit time and attention to him. Gratitude springs from the experience and belief that the other person has shared knowledge, experience, and skills—that, far from taking advantage of our limitations, the other person has used them as a starting point for helping us.

When we open ourselves to another and gain something important in return, we also feel gratitude. The other person was gracious in the presence of our vulnerability and, instead of taking advantage of us, offered something useful and important in return. Our vulnerability was our offering, and it was taken seriously. If, however, we are filled with resentment, we are unlikely to accept help, resources, or support. We believe that we deserve what we want, and that we are being victimized when we don't get it. Paradoxically, we seek help by closing down. This points to a fundamental tension we face in the transition to a post-industrial society. On the one hand, the new sensibility provides us with the tools and desires to open ourselves to others. But, on the other hand, deepening resentment propels us to shut ourselves down while undermining others. Resentment gives way to greed and the stifling conviction that we cannot gain resources unless someone else loses them. We therefore need to deeply understand how the psychodynamics of resentment can be overcome.

In the following example we explore the dynamics of resentment and how two key partners of a consulting firm overcame them and thus experienced gratitude. This gratitude, in turn, opened the way to a richer group life and to a new ability to plan for the future of the business. The example will help us see how the dynamics of resentment and gratitude are made manifest in the process of organizational development. Overcoming resentment is one of the most important challenges we face in the transition to a post-modern age.

2. See chapter 6 of Annah Segal's *Introduction to the Work of Melanie Klein* (Basic Books, 1974).

Example: Lincoln and Associates

Lincoln and Associates was a business consulting firm whose eight partners and ten associates helped small businesses develop solid financial and marketing plans in the early years of their growth. The practice was risky because, though the firm charged its clients an hourly rate for its services, its partners' bonuses and other incomes were derived largely from the success of their clients. Clients who hired them were bound by contract to pay them a fee based on their earnings over a number of years. The partners thus faced the challenge of assessing whether or not a client could in fact succeed in its market. Despite these complexities, the firm was doing well, and the partners' incomes had risen faster than they had ever imagined. Moreover, the partners brought a moral sensibility to their work. In helping small businesses, they felt, they were helping local communities establish sound economic bases at a time when many large companies were laying off employees and closing facilities. The partners held themselves to high standards. Because small businesses are vulnerable to service providers, the partners steered clear of any policies and practices that could stimulate greed, carelessness, or dishonesty. Steve, the managing partner, was a finance expert, a lawyer, and a manager of great talent. He was also the firm's principal "rainmaker"

A year before the events I will describe below, I had worked with Steve and another partner, Susan, who had then wanted Steve to delegate more authority to her, particularly for personnel matters. Susan had argued that she was effective in this area, that Steve had enough work with all the other facets of the firm's business, and that this new role would help her develop leadership skills. Steve had wanted to comply, but he had experienced enormous difficulty in giving up control. During the third session of this previous work, Steve had mentioned that when entering his office each morning he repeated a phrase from my book on teams[3]: "a culture of direct talk." He would say to himself that "direct talk" between colleagues and co-workers was an ideal from himself and the firm. As Steve described this to me, I imagined him repeating the phrase as a mantra to deflect or push away unwanted and perhaps contradictory thoughts.

3. Larry Hirschhorn, *Managing in the New Team Environment* (Addison-Wesley, 1990).

Over the course of our five sessions together, Steve and Susan agreed that Susan would take up the work of managing the firm's personnel issues; however, Steve also noted (with Susan present) that, although Susan had seemed to have enjoyed our sessions together, he had felt pained throughout. I suggested that he and I continue to work together and that I meet the other partners in the firm. Although he agreed, he dropped out of sight for nine months. He had, I believe, had enough of me and my help. He eventually called back, describing an upcoming year-end retreat for the firm's partners, which he faced with considerable anxiety.

In particular, Steve wanted the partners to think about different ways of distributing the firm's bonus money, which he was currently responsible for. Under the current procedure, Steve interviewed each partner in confidence and prepared a suggested distribution of bonus money, including his own. The partners were extremely uncomfortable talking to one another about the bonus money and depended deeply on Steve to come up with a fair result. Steve felt burdened by this process, on two accounts. First, it was difficult work. Second, because he was the key rainmaker, he often gave himself the largest bonus but felt uncomfortable in doing so. He felt entitled to the money, but he worried that if the partners objected to his recommendations it would prove that they really did not acknowledge his contributions. George, a senior partner in the firm, subsequently told me that Steve seemed to want praise and reassurance for the job he was doing.

Nearly a year earlier, when I first met Steve and Susan and described the consultation process to them, Steve said that he "worried" that he would "have the advantage" over me since he naturally knew more about the firm than I did. I said that of course he knew more about the firm, but that I would certainly know more about what was going on among the three of us. Steve's "worry" was revealing. He was afraid to dominate me, though clearly he thought he could. He was communicating to me that, in exercising power, he feared overwhelming others. If this vignette and the preceding one are connected, they suggest that Steve wanted praise because its absence meant that others experienced him as destructive.

Meanwhile, Steve was anticipating another difficulty at the retreat. He wanted to give a non-partner associate, Harriet, a significant bonus, perhaps exceeding those of some partners, because she had helped Steve collaborate with a law firm that had, on behalf of a small business client they both served, successfully sued a large company for patent infringement. The successful suit had created an unprecedented level of earnings for the firm, and Harriet had played a critical role in helping Steve develop the complex documentation required for the suit. As became clear later, Harriet expected an extremely large bonus, even though she had neither brought the case into the firm nor figured centrally in developing a strategy for supporting the law firm.

The Interviews

In preparation for the retreat, I interviewed all the firm's partners over the course of two days. They seemed to be oddly disconnected from one another, even lonely. The two most senior partners, Mike and George, appeared detached from the younger partners and seemed to play little, if any, role in leading and mentoring the "next generation." However, Steve had a somewhat different view. When he had joined the firm, Mike had, in fact, trained Steve in valuing the assets of small businesses. Steve told me that he considered Mike to be his mentor, though their relationship had long ago cooled off. Indeed, at this point, Steve was Mike's titular superior.

Mike had made an important contribution by writing a book targeted to small business owners on business planning and implementation. This book had brought significant business into the firm. Yet most of the partners felt that Mike often failed as a consultant in the field; he communicated poorly with this clients, and this seemed to be a source of continuing disappointment to him. Indeed, in my interview with him, Mike treated the operations of the firm casually—everyone else was making enough money, he noted, and he had done the best he could.

George also appeared detached and skeptical of retreat work in general; he noted that his own practice was so different from others (he focused on issues of managerial efficiency) that he hardly belonged to the firm. He worried that he was a burden on the firm. Taking into account the overhead costs, he noted, his operations ran at a loss.

The other partners appeared equally ambivalent about the retreat. Henry, a younger partner, seemed suspicious and was reluctant to join me in the room I was using for interviewing, wanting me instead to come to his office. Charles, who had been with the firm for a long time, appeared ill and uncertain. Susan alone appeared eager for the retreat; her previous work with Steve had led her to believe that such direct communication among partners in the firm could be helpful.

I too felt discouraged and uncertain after these interviews, and recommended to Steve that he not hold the retreat. I could not see the pull or drive for a group life and better collaboration, and I worried that some of the interpersonal problems appeared intractable. Steve was insistent, however. After seeking the counsel of my partner Nancy, I sat down with Steve to craft an agenda that I felt could be helpful and meet some of his minimal needs. We decided that Steve would first present the financial state of the firm, and I would then facilitate a discussion on how potential clients were selected and bonuses decided on. I invited my colleague Marilyn to join me as a co-consultant.

The Retreat

To my great surprise, the retreat was rich and provocative. Partners roamed over a wide range of issues, talking about the interpersonal processes that stymied their feelings, about the managing partner role and the business, and about organizational issues they faced. Among this array of issues and themes, two emerged as fundamental: Steve's sense of being burdened (particularly by his role in distributing bonuses) and his ambivalent relationship to Mike (he resented him yet also wanted his acknowledgment and attention).

Steve's burden
Steve's sense of burden played a central role in shaping the dynamics of the retreat. Not only was he the managing partner; he was the only one who really understood deeply the legal dimensions of both the clients' and the partners' situations. In addition, he was the main rainmaker, and he had to allocate bonuses to peers and colleagues. He wanted relief, yet his resentment made it difficult for him to accept relief when it might be offered.

For example, while the partners had a rich discussion on how they as a group could more effectively control which clients any partner chose to accept, Steve argued that they had been too careless in this regard and had lost considerable money because their initial valuations were too optimistic. It was not so much that the clients failed as that the profits they returned were too small to create significant earnings for the firm. The partners agreed and remembered that they had once met to discuss this issue but had failed to come up with a resolution. Yet, as the discussion unfolded, it be came clear that their client-selection practices reflected a fragmented partnership. Each partner worried about his or her *own* utilization. They would take clients with dubious potential to stay active—to be billable—even if that meant forgoing better though less frequently appearing opportunities. Moreover, this process was self-fulfilling. Insofar as each partner was kept busy by a larger number of marginal clients, he or she could not overcome the sense of insecurity that business was slipping away. As one partner, John, said: "I think, 'if I am going to turn down this client down, will I lose future business?' This entire train of consequences made it harder for the group as a whole to slow down and take clients that had the potential of being very profitable." John noted poignantly: "I could give up the idea of these marginal clients. It is so hard, though, for I know I can always earn my keep with them. I am so used to making something out of nothing."

I felt that the conversation was promising; people were beginning to acknowledge their role in client selection. However, just at this point Steve attacked the group: "People come to me and complain that we are not following the client selection method that we already agreed to. And the people that complain are the people I see ignoring it themselves." He then asked "Are people really committed to this?"—implying that he believed they were not. The group sat in silence, as if they had no choice but to accept Steve's anger. I asked "When Steve says 'Are you committed?' do people think they can never satisfy him?" No one answered.

I felt that a productive conversation had turned into an arena for threats and fear. Steve had enunciated a vague threat—it was as if he had said "I can identify the dishonest among you." People had seemed to accept this in silence. Their fundamental dependency on him was now apparent (after all, if he left the firm it would probably collapse), and they would not challenge him. It appears as if, in the process itself, Steve had said to his partners "If you start to support me I will increase the heat on all of you." This suggests that Steve's irritation had roots in something other than his dissatisfaction with his partners. Their prospective cooperation brought these other feelings closer to awareness. He relished his resentment of them.

This insight was buttressed by the group's discussion of Harriet's bonus. Steve made a strong case for giving Harriet a sizable amount of money. Though he did not mention a specific figure, he pointed out how much she supported him: she arranged his graphical presentations, organized his documents, and facilitated the writing of his reports. The partners respond skeptically, noting that she did not operate independently of him—why should she then be so richly rewarded?

As the discussion continued, people became increasingly hostile to Harriet. They reflected on her history with the firm and the "just rewards" she had received so far; they resented her sense of "entitlement." They pressed Steve to tell them what Harriet in fact wanted, and after some coyness he said "$100,000 to $250,000." The partners laughed in amazement—even I was drawn into the uproar. Steve then said he would agree to give Harriet $75,000, but the partners argued that this was too much.

What was going on here? Steve seemed to be acting realistically. After all, just as Susan had taken up some of the work of managing the firm, Harriet had supported Steve's high-profile work with the law firm in the patent-infringement case. However, I believe there was an irrational aspect to this process. Steve did not have to tell the partners what Harriet had requested. He knew it was too large a sum—hence his coyness. He could have devised tactics to support a reasonable raise for her without exposing her to ridicule. It was as if he wanted the partners to deny Harriet the bonus she wanted—not because he wished to hurt her, but because he wished to create a conflict about what rewards *he* was entitled to. In a manner that resonated with George's characterization of Steve's need for praise, Steve was actually saying to his partners "Prove to me that you really acknowledge my contributions to the firm." By setting so high a price, he guaranteed that he would not be acknowledged; however, he justified his continued resentment of his colleagues and his belief that they did not understand how burdened he was.

The partners agreed to vote on the size of Harriet's bonus. They submitted their proposals to Marilyn on paper ballots, and it turned out that a large majority of the partners wanted to give Harriet $50,000. At this point, Steve made a revealing slip of the tongue. He turned to the group and said that if the partners preferred it, he would gladly agree to give her $75,000! While everyone laughed at the way he had misspoken, Steve appeared puzzled. When I pointed out his "slip," he, embarrassed, said emphatically "Well, I give up"—as if to say "Well you got me here, I don't know what I am doing." This highlighted some of the dynamics Steve was wrestling with. His slip was a "deep" one. Most people recognize a slip as they make it and correct themselves. Steve's failure to notice his slip, even after others laughed at it, signified that deep currents of feeling had been tapped. Steve stated that he would accede to the group's wishes, but through his slip of the tongue he revealed the opposite: that he would *not* accede to those wishes. This was reminiscent of his earlier mantra-like repetition of the phrase "a culture of direct talk." He believed that he *should* comply with his partners' wishes, but in fact he did not want to.

Steve and I subsequently discussed this event, and he told me that he had learned that he "should back off." I was surprised at his conclusion and told him so. If the retreat had proved anything, it was that Steve and his partners were able to collaborate in assessing the firm's management issues. I felt that his response was petulant— as if the work of the retreat itself had been punishing. His slip of the tongue revealed the pain he was experiencing: he felt that he was being pushed, against his will, to comply with partners' requests that he experienced resentfully as demands.

Authority and gratitude

As I have noted, resentment and gratitude are linked to authority relations. In early life, a child can feel gratitude toward her parents or older siblings if she internalizes these authority figures as nurturing as well as demanding. In this situation the harsh character of these demands is softened by feelings that one is being nurtured, respected, and loved. Demands appear as instruments of education rather than as punishment, while the sense of gratitude and appreciation redounds to the individual's self-esteem. The internal psychological statement becomes "I am being asked to subordinate myself because I have been judged to be worthy by a person whom I deeply appreciate and respect."

Casting the above internal psychological statement in such a way highlights what a momentous achievement this kind of relationship to authority represents. In addition, there can be many missteps blocking the evolution of such a relationship. Individuals with fragile self-esteem—the result, for example, of inadequate parenting—may be unable to believe that they are capable of discipline and achievement. They may desire the love and protection of the authority figure but feel helpless in meeting his or her demands. In this case, the authority relationship can lead to a lifelong wish to be dependent on others and a disbelief in one's capacity for self-reliance. Similarly, one can project feelings of unworthiness onto the authority figure. The authority figure (teacher, mentor, superior) then becomes an object of contempt whose interests in teaching, instructing, and disciplining are resented.

I hypothesize that Steve experienced authority as insufficiently loving and uncaring. People with considerable gifts and talents can develop their competence in the face of hostile or indifferent parents, but they are likely to have unsettled relationships with the authority figures of their adult lives. They resent the authority figure for being, in the transference, the ungiving parent; but they also wish and hope that the authority figure will finally love the once-disregarded child. Under these conditions, a person may offer his competence as signifying that he is worthy of love. This helps explain Steve's apparent need for reassurance that he was indeed important to the firm. Steve, I suggest, found himself in just such a situation. He was highly competent, people admired his talents and skills, he got the lion's share of the bonus, but he still felt unacknowledged. That is why he felt viscerally that being denied what he wanted meant he had been rejected by his partners. Yet Steve was sensitive to his own struggle. His neediness irked him because it contrasted with the adult parts of his makeup. He wanted a culture of direct talk; he wanted to cooperate with his partners; he wanted to share his own authority. These feelings represented genuine aspirations. That is why he faced considerable pain in trying to reconstruct his role. He came up against fundamental conflicts.

Mike

The most important moment of the retreat consisted of a profound exchange between Steve and Mike. Steve had described Mike as his mentor, and Mike had told the story of how he had championed Steve's bid to become a partner. "I went to my partners," Mike noted, "and I told them, 'We have got to hire this guy; we better hire this guy.'"

When I first interviewed Mike, he projected an air of nonchalance that seemed to express a conviction that he had settled his score with life. His relationship to the firm, and to his own role within the firm, was relaxed to the point of detachment. At the same time, he occupied an important position—old enough to be linked to the generation that started the firm and young enough still to be practicing—and he had written an important book. He told me how a Buddhist teacher had helped him see that he had done the best he could. To be sure, such feelings seem quite appropriate in an older man, but I felt that in Mike they highlighted a sense of irresponsibility to his younger partners. In their early forties, these partners were naturally concerned about how much money they made; however, Mike expressed a contempt for money and could not understand why people wanted it and why they raced after it. I could not understand why he did not honor young people's need for money. To me this felt ungenerous, ungiving.

Furthermore, Steve had reported that Mike lost money for the firm. Several times he had advised Mike not to take on a certain client but Mike had done so anyway—and had then failed to tell Steve. Mike's nonchalance, or carelessness, played counterpoint to what people described as his "drivenness" in the area of marketing: Mike was proud of his book, as he should have been, but too frequently he came up with marketing schemes and suggestions that seemed to his partners impulsive and insufficiently considered. It seemed that Mike's studied detachment may have partly masked a sense that he had yet to prove his worth.

The contrast between Mike and George is interesting. George seemed to be at peace with his accomplishments, worrying primarily that he might no longer be a productive member of the firm. Interestingly, eight months after the retreat, when the firm contacted me once again, George, rather than Steve, took up the liaison role. I felt then as if the retreat had sufficiently grounded him in the firm, and that he felt able to provide some leadership because he had no special interest to promote.

Mike and Steve

Mike resisted Steve's authority not in order to usurp his role (Mike certainly did not want to manage anybody) but in order to remain free of Steve's influence and direction. At the retreat, when discussing what a managing partner's role should be, Mike said "We are all equals, and the managing partner is just an administrative role." Steve countered, in effect, that the managing partner does have significant power, and he was unwilling to give it up. However, his voice trailed off, and he backed away from confronting Mike.

Subsequently, at lunch, Marilyn briefly suggested to Steve that he and Mike had much work to do in building a better working relationship with each other. After lunch, during a "hot" discussion of bonuses, Steve turned to Mike, on the edge of tears; he fixed on him and said: "This is between you and me. We have to work it out between us in private. But this needs to be said in the group. Do I mind your approach to me? Yes. Do I care about you? Yes." Mike protested weakly—as if to say "What could this mean?"—but then settled into listening and looking. I believe that Steve's eloquent words represented a "love letter" to Mike. Interestingly, after this interaction the afternoon's work slowed down. It seemed as if the group had accomplished an important piece of work.

What was going on here? I suggest that Mike and Steve were locked in a vicious circle. Steve felt that Mike had been his mentor and wanted his respect and acknowledgment. Instead, he felt that Mike disregarded him and undermined him, as if Mike could not take him seriously as a colleague. Mike, however, did not *want* to be a senior statesman, freed from the burdens of ambitions and thus able to support young colleagues. He was detached from the firm and its partners—perhaps as a way of avoiding his still-incomplete evaluation of his own work and contributions. Mike was not ready to be and act generatively—that is, to abandon his hold on the future by investing in younger people who would outlive him. Indeed, in an afternoon discussion during the retreat, Mike reminisced poignantly about what it had been like as a young associate in the firm: "I landed my first big contract, so I went to the my favorite bar by myself to celebrate what I had accomplished." In others words, he had felt the sting of being ignored by his elders. One reason he could not give support and praise was that he had not received enough of it. Steve, in turn, interpreted Mike's withdrawal as a sign that Mike did not regard Steve seriously, did not value his contribution, and did not care about his feelings. Steve, therefore, grew more resentful and needy, and Mike, responding to this pressure, withdrew further. This helps explain Steve's chronic dissatisfaction. Thinking of this in family terms, one might say that Steve was transferring onto Mike feelings he had about having missed a father who was loving while also exercising discipline. In other words, Steve could not accept Mike for what he was; instead he tried to turn him into an unloving father. This helps explain his chronic grumpiness.

The above analysis sheds light on why Steve considered bonuses so important. He both produced the largest profits for the firm and was in charge of awarding bonuses based on these profits to each partner. The dilemmas this created for Steve were quite apparent; indeed, he was quite conscious of them himself. However, this analysis points to a deeper current of feeling linked to Steve's relationships to Mike. Steve, we might say, lacked a "good enough" internalized image of a father who both disciplines and loves his son. This suggests that the psychodynamic meaning of Steve's rewarding himself—of providing himself with his own sustenance and support (e.g., Harriet)—might be interpreted as Steve's becoming his own father.

Psychoanalysis puts much store in a son's struggle with his father, and it is useful to look at Mike and Steve through Freud's interpretation of the drama of Oedipus. Today we often use the term "Oedipus complex" too loosely, imagining that it means simply a son's wish to possess his mother and defeat his father. However, as the term "self-made man" suggests, the oedipal son, by lying with the mother, fathers himself. Thinking in mythical terms, we say that he no longer depends on anyone for his existence. Since the Oedipus story is in fact a tragedy, we can also say that this wish to father oneself leads to a profound state of dependency: the blinded son has little control over anything.

This mythical interpretation provides significant insight into Steve's struggles. Rejected by a mentor, he had learned to father himself; as a consequence, he was alone and isolated, deeply dependent on the acknowledgment and praise of others. By sending Mike his spoken "love letter," he began to overcome his resentment. He softened the phrase "Do I mind your approach to me?" (which bespeaks resentment) with "Do I care about you?" (which bespeaks love). This moment completed the group's work for the day because the contact between Mike and Steve had reduced the anxiety and tension everyone had been feeling. The stage had now been set for Mike and Steve to acknowledge what each had given the other.

Results of the retreat

In the face of the difficulties noted above, the group had made significant progress. People were surprised at their ability to work effectively with one another and to bring important issues to the surface. They were proud of their work, and they appreciated the pool of talent and resources they represented. The end of the retreat felt calm and contained, and people sat quietly as they contemplated leaving. One young partner noted at the end: "At first I didn't expect much from the retreat. I did not think that someone could tell me what I feel, but now I see that I can tell what I feel." Mike said that he wanted to take more of a part in the firm's activities. Later he said to me "If the retreat meant anything to me, it's that Steve and I understood each other."

The partners used a different process for distributing bonuses that year—they allocated bonus money as a group rather than using Steve as a go-between. There was some dissatisfaction with this new process. Some people felt that group decision making made it difficult for the partners to deny someone a bonus. Nine months later (when I was engaged by the firm for a third time to do some work), one partner told me that he did not deserve the bonus he got and would prefer not to be indulged but rather to be treated more as a professional. They also developed a new client-selection system based on the simple idea that a partner's letter of agreement with a potential client had to be countersigned by another partner.

As I approached this third phase of my work with the firm, George took up the role of being my liaison, so Steve was no longer in the middle. This role proved difficult for George, but I was struck by his willingness to take it up.

My work with the firm continues. After a third retreat, conducted by my co-consultant, the firm decided to undertake business planning. Though successful, the firm as a whole had never formally planned its own business, depending instead on the talents and energies of the individual partners. Yet the environment for the firm's work was changing. A rising stock market offered small businesses new sources of capital, daughters were playing stronger roles in managing family businesses, and big companies were selecting fewer suppliers (often small businesses) but treating them more favorably than in the past. Steve, George, and Susan constituted a business planning committee and created the first forum where the implications for these changes could be addressed without generating undue anxiety. At the first meeting, for example, they wrestled with the question of how to evaluate business opportunities without at the same time evaluating each partner's past decisions and practices. The partners' preoccupation with the firm's internal workings and relationships are receding, and they have begun to focus on outside threats and opportunities. All this suggests that the partners had in fact been able to do some repair work, to reduce the transferences they imposed on one another, and to see each other realistically, with appreciation and gratitude.

In sum

People's ability to open up to one another at work is shaped deeply by the psychodynamics of authority, resentment, and gratitude. Gratitude rests on a person's belief that the difficulties he or she has experienced with another person are part and parcel of contributions the other person has made to his or her own activities and accomplishments. Such feelings of gratitude can help contain the resentment that often comes from being subordinate to or dependent on someone. When such feelings are absent, either because the subordinate simply cannot feel appreciative or because the superior demonstrates a lack of care and concern, chronic conflict emerges.

The failure of Steve's relationship with Mike, his mentor, had kept him from taking up his own role effectively. Instead, he had wanted to be admired and acknowledged. Feeling unappreciated, he had interpreted his leadership tasks as burdens and had come to resent them. In turn, his colleagues had experienced him as someone who simply could not be satisfied. These dynamics had significantly impaired the ability of the partners to function as a cohesive business team. They could not develop a coherent client-acquisition policy, they could not design a bonus system that would be good enough, and they did not engage in business planning.

The retreat provided a starting point for working through these issues. Most important, Steve and Mike "understood each other better," and this established a basis for moments of reconciliation and development for the partnership as a whole. Resentment was softened by the stirrings of gratitude. Can this be a general model for repairing the insults and injuries brought on by the transition to a post-modern world?

Conclusion: Building a Culture of Openness

Resentment not only divides us from others; it also estranges us from the sources of our authority. A resenting person or group is locked into psychological dependency on the person resented—a dependency that limits the resenting person's ability to negotiate with authority for a different relationship.

A sense of failure can breed resentment. In the case of Lincoln and Associates (chapter 7), Steve's sense of failure appeared to be based on early disappointments in his life. Although objectively Steve had succeeded, Mike's lack of acknowledgment meant that he had failed. Resentment feeds on itself. An individual who resents others feels victimized. Feeling victimized, that individual feels even weaker, and this breeds more resentment. Overcoming resentment is a twofold process. First, a resenting individual or group must overcome the sense of isolation. Victims feel exiled from the human community. They are ashamed of their ineffectiveness and their inability to exercise choice. Second, a resenting individual must take personal risks to revitalize himself. Granted success feels hollow and leaves the grantee a supplicant. Resenters need help in forging their own success.

To contain and soften feelings of resentment, a human community must create an ethic of forgiveness—of second and third chances. Members of a community cannot let earlier failures undermine the hope that a psychological sense of community can reemerge, that estrangement can be overcome, that an individual's exile has been rescinded. Expressions of forgiveness must flow in three directions: the victim must forgive himself; the victim must forgive his real or imagined oppressors; and individuals who have succeeded must forgive those who, in their failure, once appeared contemptible and dishonored. In forgiving ourselves and others, we become a fair society by focusing less on who was responsible for past failures and more on our shared accountability for recovering and rebuilding.

But the hope for forgiveness may feel utopian. Politics is often about the fairness of past decisions: who sacrificed too much, who deserves recompense. Politics makes resentment the center of feelings. To counter resentment, to attenuate its force, we must develop social policies that help sustain a climate of forgiveness and give both victims and victimizers new chances. We affirm our psychological sense of community in practical ways through the social policies we develop and implement.

The post-modern organization plays contradictory roles here. When individuals lose their jobs, their life plans are undermined and their resentment grows. On the other hand, individuals working in a post-modern organization can deepen their sense of authority, learn that economic and technological risks make everyone vulnerable, and experience how a group becomes more secure when individuals become more open to one another by acknowledging their relatedness. The paradoxical nature of the post-modern organization—it is both a transmission belt for fragmentation and disruption and a crucible for the development of a psychological sense of community—poses two challenges: We must learn how to contain the tensions the paradox creates, and we must develop wider social policies that ameliorate them. In this concluding chapter I explore how, with good design and management, the post-modern organization can help individuals recover their authority and build a psychological sense of community; I also consider how social policies can help safeguard these accomplishments.

The Current Context

The economic context for such a social policy appears inhospitable. Today it seems that companies have never been more careless about the people they employ: layoffs, closings, and consolidations have put an end to presumed careers and long-held jobs throughout the economy. In such a context it appears foolish to predict or even hope for a wider culture that promotes openness. The current corporate environment seems hostile to it.

Psychological pain and economic hardship characterize the current experience of work. Although corporate elites have profited from this pain and hardship, it is too one-sided to imagine that these results derive simply from corporate greed. Pain and hardship can also be elements of a developmental process.

As firms enter a post-industrial economy, they must indeed remake themselves—inherited career ladders, skills profiles, and the management of information must all change dramatically. To thrive, firms cannot only cut costs; by developing new products and services, modifying systems to produce them, and creating new market channels for their distribution, they must also develop new sources of revenue. For this latter reason they will come to depend increasingly on employees' commitment and creativity. When a company faces this moment in its development, it must in one way or another confront the challenge of building a culture of greater openness—not, as some gurus would promise, because executives want to humanize their companies, but because it is the most practical alternative.

This is the contradiction that firm now faces: it must construct a nimble and flexible enterprise that provides employees with less job security; yet the employees must feel secure enough to share information, skills, and feelings with one another in order to create this nimble, flexible enterprise. In short, the enterprise must comprise a culture of openness. How is this possible? I want to explore three avenues for resolving this contradiction: the rewards the flexible enterprise grants its employees, the role that social policies can play in reducing employees' sense of security, and the role that wider cultural changes play in changing what is valued.

The Rewards of Flexibility

Career security imposes its own hidden costs. Post-World War II social critics examined the price people paid for career stability. Most often, this stability entailed the pain of conforming to a company's code of behavior. Employees were taught to not "rock the boat"; they were to dress appropriately, to suppress their spontaneity, to repress their feelings, to participate in staged meetings, and to focus on the organizational underground where cabals and coalitions were formed and rumors were created. The cultural revolution of the

1960s was aimed precisely at this configuration of experience, this corporate way of life.

Career security thus had its price. The firm promised to protect its employees from the market, but only if the employee surrendered substantial individuality. This was the crucible of the "psychological contract" between firms and employees from the end of World War II until the early 1970s. The firm protected its loyal (i.e., "conforming") employees, while unions protected many blue-collar workers from managers' arbitrary decisions.

Corporate paternalism thus had paradoxical effects. By providing job security, it attenuated in part the instrumental and unforgiving market of late-nineteenth-century and early-twentieth-century industrial society. Moreover, by enforcing conformity, companies could use standardized roles and procedures to reduce cost and variability. But paternalism stimulated a particular form of authority relationship: having relinquished their capacity for thought to others, people in corporations lacked the experience, conviction, and rewards that would have accrued from developing their personal authority by collaborating with others.

As we move from the industrial economy to a post-industrial economy, we see just the reverse happening. *As companies shed paternalism, they no longer protect their employees from the market; yet they are personalizing work.* By building teams, fostering creativity, and promoting self-management, companies hope to draw on the inner and often latent strengths of group life. The work group can stimulate its members' creativity, it helps them build trust by offering opportunities for collaboration, and it fosters self-regulation and learning because people feel more responsible for the accomplishments of their work. The following questions then arise: How and why and when do people feel that this exchange is beneficial to them? Will they accept it? Will that acceptance help firms transform their current chaotic organizational processes into creative ones?

Organizational Development

To assess the issues, it is useful to review briefly the history of organizational development in the United States. Three phases are important.

The first phase, which began before World War II but was given particular emphasis by the "quality of work life" movement in the

1970s, helped create a more considerate workplace wherein managers treated subordinates with less callousness and senior executives systematically assessed and took account of employees' opinions on a wide range of organizational issues. In this same period increasing numbers of managers attended management training programs delivered by consulting companies and business schools. Once derided as "charm schools," these programs were taken more seriously as senior executives faced a rash of new human-relations problems, including discrimination in hiring and promotion, the role of women in the workplace, and blue-collar discontent. Many executives sponsored these programs, and the efforts at organizational change they stimulated, in order to reduce workers' complaints and thus the power of unions.

In the 1980s the second phase unfolded. Confronting competitors from Japan, other Asian countries, and Europe, senior executives found the costs of their operations too high and the quality of their products and services too low. Influenced by Edward Deming (the "father" of quality control), by Japanese production methods, and by methods for promoting self-managing or loosely managed worker teams, companies deployed workers to help in restructuring the production of goods and services. Managers no longer sought to placate workers or to limit the impact of their discontent. Instead they mobilized them to reshape and redesign the work. Workers interacted more frequently with engineers and customers, and managers were more often deployed on cross-functional teams to solve market problems. In both of these phases, work was more personalized. Women could emerge from the stereotyped roles that limited their self-expression, and all workers could interact more freely with authority figures and more fully with co-workers.

Now a third phase has begun to unfold. Many companies and other organizations are beginning to emerge from the cost-cutting phase. Some, like IBM, are now re-hiring. With their operations restructured and their costs reduced, organizations must now determine how to raise revenues by developing and selling new or modified products and services. The contours of this phase are not yet defined, but I want to suggest that in this phase organizations face the challenge of including employees in discussions of strategy. To help them discover consumers' emergent needs, design products for them, and get customers' feedback on the quality and usability of the products, employees must be given, and must themselves develop, a better understanding what the company's goals are and how the firm expects to gain revenue in the future.

Each phase personalizes work more deeply and brings the organization closer to creating a culture of openness. In the first phase managers were sensitized to the role of feelings in shaping a climate for work. In the second, managers and employees learned to mobilize their feelings so as to engage in the work of restructuring. And in the third, managers and employees link their feelings to the primary risks of the enterprise, and thus to its future. In each phase, the "emotion work"[1] becomes more intense and more deeply connected to the tasks and performance of the enterprise.

Strategy Work

Companies alone cannot create the post-modern enterprise. Broad cultural trends play an important role, and the politics of the transition period will prove formative. Within their sphere of action, however, senior executives can develop an enterprise so that it engages feelings at a deeper level. This suggests, in this context, that to shape the post-modern enterprise senior executives must increasingly engage employees in strategy work. What obstacles are firms are likely to face here, and how can their executives contribute to their post-modernization?

Strategy work cannot be located in one division, one location, or one work station. Instead, as business theorists suggest, strategy is *enacted*. It takes place as influential executives throughout the organization test new ideas, invest in projects, and compete for development money. The chief executive officer can exercise different degrees of influence over this process. If the CEO has a very clear vision of the company's strategy—e.g., Sam Walton's original strategy of "building big stores in little towns"—then he or his subordinates can enact their strategies within narrow limits. When the CEO lacks such a vision, strategy decisions are made through ongoing negotiations among coalitions of executives.

Ironically, while strategy emerges from a negotiation process, executives, when self-consciously "doing strategy," have often resorted to

---

1. See Arlie Russell Hochschild, *The Managed Heart: Commercialization of Human Feeling* (University of California Press, 1983).

using formal methods in highly structured settings. For example, in the 1960s and the 1970s some companies developed "strategic planning" departments composed of experts in finance and marketing who produced strategic plans for ratification by the CEO and the board. Research has suggested that these departments were strikingly without influence and that their plans went unimplemented.[2] In retrospect it is clear that these departments ritualized planning as a way of containing the real anxiety and the real work of negotiating for the company's future. Just as totalitarian countries sponsored pseudo-elections to disguise the sources of real political decisions, these planning departments produced pseudo-plans to keep underground the political conflicts, interpersonal skirmishes, and serendipitous actions that shaped actual strategy.

In my experience, when a team of executives uses a formal process the members suppress their thinking and the team creates flat and uninspiring plans. Strategy discussions among executives provoke much anxiety. Every systematic discussion of the future entails some assessment of the past, and each executive feels personally at risk when participating in such discussions. Once, when working with a hospital's executive team, I and my colleagues witnessed the deep personal stakes the members faced. Chronic interpersonal conflicts surfaced, people were keenly aware that any decision would reshape the members' work and responsibilities differentially, they worried about powerful political groups not included in the discussion (e.g., physicians), and they were keenly aware that their legitimacy depended on their ability to communicate the reasons for their decisions simply and without pretense. In my own group's judgment, the executives failed. They wrestled unsuccessfully with the balance between cutting costs and raising revenues, and they postponed rather than resolved many issues. This points to a general rule of thumb for understanding these processes: *High-stakes strategic issues stimulate executives to use more formal planning methods. These methods, in turn, create more superficial discussions and less meaningful decisions.* The formal methods function as a social defense against the anxieties stimulated by the strategic issues.

In this context, I believe that executives must learn to have what I call "strategic conversations" with one another and with their

2. See Henry Mintzberg, *The Rise and Fall of Strategic Planning* (Free Press, 1994).

subordinates. Such conversations, while supported by data and by rigorous thinking (*thinking*, not planning), should be as freewheeling as possible. Members should attend to the content of their conversation but also to its process. In particular, members should want to learn how apparently interpersonal differences and tensions reflect underlying strategic tensions that face the enterprise as whole. Today, when responding to difficult personal encounters in a meeting, members often describe them in personal terms: "X does not like Y," or "Z is afraid of W." Aware of the spectators who have gathered to watch them fight, they take up the roles assigned to them in this public performance, if only to look tough and save face. Yet often these roles emerge because they represent strategic choices that all executives must confront.

For example, I once worked with a small publishing company that produced specialized texts accompanied by guidebooks intended to help teachers introduce primary school students to important works of history and literature written for adults. The executive team was rife with conflict, ostensibly because several executives disliked one another intensely. Yet as I began to help the team it became apparent that these differences represented deep-seated anxieties about their product's viability in a changing school environment. Future sales were at stake. But rather than face these issues, team members were content to translate them into the familiar and time-worn stories of power relationships between people and between groups. Academics and journalists who study and report on such conflicts imagine that they are being tough-minded when they see behind the polite rhetoric of planning to the "real" underlying conflicts over power, but in fact these power conflicts are as unreal as the planning rhetoric. They are only encoded representations of the strategic anxieties every team member faces. The team's choices, which make vivid the relationships between the enterprise and its environment, stimulate the conflicts and tensions among the team's members.

The strategic conversation is emblematic of the next phase of organizational development. Although its particular form and range of application cannot be predicted, as an "ideal type" it represents a response to the newest challenges facing the post-modern organization. This sheds light on the culture of openness I have described throughout this book. I have emphasized that the main risk facing the enterprise—and, by implication, the strategic choices these risks illuminate-gives the culture of openness its purpose. To face their vulnerability to these risks, and the strategies they illuminate, I have argued, leaders and followers must become more open, more vulnerable to one another. If they cannot, they become obstacles to one another and more susceptible to events in the market.

Rewards Again

It is my belief that the above-mentioned developments in the structure and culture of organizations have conferred unambiguous benefits on employees and on the firms they work in. They allow people to be more psychologically present at work, less alienated from their own experiences. People's opportunities for learning increase (both on the job and in educational programs), and they can develop the personal roots of their own authority. They are engaged more in the tasks of the enterprise and less in the politics. Yet it remains reasonable to ask whether these gains are worth the loss of security that the employees experience. After all, the same economic processes that stimulate teamwork have also increased job instability and reduced people's sense of the organization's coherence.

The Political Level

Political and social policies must play roles in increasing the benefits and decreasing the costs of working in the post-modern organization. As I have noted, organizations face the paradox of integrating their employees more deeply into the work process while eliminating job security. We can critique a firm's policy and hope to rein in what appears to be the elite executives' greed. But it also seems evident that there are limits, in a capitalistic society, on what companies alone can do to ensure their employees stable lives, their customers good products, and their shareholders or stakeholders profits or institutional solvency and program success.

Government must protect employees from the dark side of post-industrialism. While many people talk today of the social safety net as if it were only for the poor, increasing numbers of employees, professionals, and managers are being "proletarianized" and feel unsafe. Under these conditions we can only expect that they will approach their work, their colleagues and co-workers, and their employers warily. A social stalemate is emerging here. In a climate of competitiveness and cost reduction, corporations support the cutting of taxes and of government spending. Yet, in the absence of a new government-supported social safety net, employees will be too anxious to take the personal and organizational risks required to keep companies competitive.

We need a new, post-industrial safety net. In a risky society, such a safety net would provide people with second and third chances, with opportunities to develop in the face of failure. It would assure people of health care, it would help people retool and learn new skills, it would help people create enterprises as well as join them, and it would require that a person receiving help share in the risks of securing this help.

First, the new safety net would eliminate some of the anxieties as well as some of the real risks people face when they lose or switch jobs.

Second, the new safety net would not simply support "retraining programs," which are often focused too narrowly on jobs or skills that may disappear; it would support education that helps people develop their learning skills.

Third, the new safety net would acknowledge that in the post-industrial economy large corporations have a different role than in the past. They are less centers of production and more centers of financing—that is, organizational instruments through which owners and executives raise large sums of capital to fund the enormous investments needed to build a post-industrial economic infrastructure. At the same time, the declining cost and increasing effectiveness of computer technology allows smaller enterprises to flourish. No longer dependent on economies of scale to keep costs low, they now generate more jobs than the large corporations. With help, people could build enterprises rather than find jobs, thus securing their future by taking rather than avoiding risks.

Fourth, with the new safety net individuals would take the risks associated with entering programs of help and development. As the post-industrial economy creates ever greater risks for firms and enterprises as well as for individuals, no social policy can hope to quash these risks. Such policies would prove too costly, and they would benefit current job holders rather than job seekers (this has been one source of high unemployment in Europe). New social policies would, in this sense, discourage "dependency" not in the simple-minded sense that people would be forced to scavenge for food or work at minimum-wage jobs (without helping people acquire the necessities of life no social policy can succeed), but in the sense that they would help people grapple with and manage the personal risks they face as they search for productive work roles. In turn, the confidence people would gain from finding such roles would enable them to contribute more effectively to the enterprises they would work in.

As I have noted, the ethic of such a social policy system would be one of second chances and forgiveness. It would be based on a more subtle understanding of risk than is represented in the old system of social policy. In the old system, we hoped to either eliminate risk (e.g., to guarantee employment) or to support the obvious "victims" (e.g., by giving laid-off workers unemployment compensation). Today, in contrast, the social and personal roots of failure are inter- twined. Individuals are at risk both because of what they have done (or failed to do) and because of what has happened to them. The dis- tinction between those who have failed and those who have been victimized is no longer self-evident. In giving people second chances, we are concerned less with who is accountable for their failure and more with their accountability to recover from it.

Readers aware of the current hostility to government may regard the hope for such a safety net as utopian. A historical perspective is helpful here. Ever since market society overturned traditional com- munities, economic development has been characterized by both ex- tension and regulation of markets. In the nineteenth century, laws forbidding child labor and limiting the length of the working day contained the impacts of the "pure" labor market. In the twentieth century, laws regulating product safety, environmental safety, and workplace safety have also helped contain that damage that unfet- tered markets create. To be sure such, regulations did not emerge au- tomatically; they resulted from significant social and political conflict. But these conflicts themselves point to a community's deep-seated wish to protect itself from the market while simultane- ously using its dynamism to advance living standards. Despite this history, current ideological discussion pretends that we face stark alternatives between regulating and extending markets. In truth, we face the more realistic task of integrating the two processes.

The Cultural Umbrella

As I noted in chapter 6, organizations can develop a culture of open-ness only if broader cultural changes support and are consonant with such a culture. People will value vulnerability not because employers ask for it but because the orientation it sustains is felt to be the moral way to work with others. Yet there is little doubt that in this transition many people feel dislocated rather than linked to a wider system of social relationships and cultural meaning. One's profession, one's employer, and one's residence are eroding as signs of one's identity. This is one reason why people have, increasingly, sought solace as well as inspiration in their ethnic or religious iden-tities, which are less susceptible than their work identities to the de-structive impacts of corporate decisions.

We face here a central tension between superficial awareness and understanding in depth. The personalization of work has the poten-tial to bring each of us to an understanding in depth of our own and our institutions' purposes, of the institutional environment that shapes them, and of the capacities and intentions of the people we work with. But, as our identities erode, we find meaning only at the surface of events. We identify with celebrities and with the psy-chodramatic elements of political life. We join a new system of meaning-making, but it is one that lays only a minimal claim on our capacity to delve into experience. As the worlds of celebrity, poli-tics, and advertising converge, we consume images and fantasies rather than products or services. The latter may represent the invest-ments we make and the risks we take in shaping identities for our-selves and our families; the former represents the identities we purchase to ensure that we can feel glamorous, if only vicariously. People living in such a world cannot bring the depths of their own experience to their work. It appears that the only antidote to this is the work experience. If work creates opportunities for relating in depth to others, and if in preparing for work we recover our own personal authority, then we can create the self-fulfilling conditions for a new culture of work. This new culture, infused with the new sensibility, may protect us from isolation and self-estrangement.

Index